# Tell Australia Goodbye?
## You've Got to be kidding!

A Moore Family Odyssey, Book Four
# Connie Moore

Epic Press

Belleville, Ontario, Canada

# TELL AUSTRALIA GOODBYE? YOU'VE GOT TO BE KIDDING!
Copyright © 2005, Connie Moore

*All Rights Reserved. No part of this publication may be reproduced, stored in a retrieval system or transmitted in any form or by any means—electronic, mechanical, photocopy, recording or any other—except for brief quotations in printed reviews, without the prior permission of the author.*

**Library and Archives Canada Cataloguing in Publication**

Moore, Connie, 1930-
  Tell Australia goodbye? You've got to be kidding! / Connie Moore.
(A Moore family odyssey ; Bk. 4)
ISBN 1-55306-997-8
ISBN 1-55306-999-4 (LSI ed.)

  1. Australia--Description and travel. 2. Moore, Connie, 1930- --Travel--United States. I. Title. II. Series: Moore, Connie, 1930- Moore Family odyssey ; Bk. 4.
DU117.2.M66A3 2005      919.404'62      C2005-906640-7


*Epic Press* is an imprint of *Essence Publishing*, a Christian Book Publisher dedicated to furthering the work of Christ through the written word. For more information, contact:
20 Hanna Court, Belleville, Ontario, Canada K8P 5J2
Phone: 1-800-238-6376 • Fax: (613) 962-3055
E-mail: publishing@essencegroup.com
Internet: www.essencegroup.com

Printed in Canada
by

# Table of Contents

*Meet the Family* . . . . . . . . . . . . . . . .5
*Preface* . . . . . . . . . . . . . . . . . . . .9
*Prologue* . . . . . . . . . . . . . . . . . .11

1. Counting Our Blessings . . . . . . . .15
2. Accidents Happen . . . . . . . . . . . .25
3. We Go By Boat . . . . . . . . . . . . . .35
4. Oh No, Not Again! . . . . . . . . . . .43
5. Learning to Cope . . . . . . . . . . . .49
6. Adventures in the Big City . . . . . .57
7. New Horizons . . . . . . . . . . . . . .65
8. Looking Ahead . . . . . . . . . . . . . .71
9. Surprise! Surprise! . . . . . . . . . . . .79
10. Mickey Grows Up . . . . . . . . . . .87
11. Summer Travel, Summer TV . . . .93
12. The Gift of Time . . . . . . . . . . . .99
13. A New Journey . . . . . . . . . . . .105
14. Hello America! . . . . . . . . . . . .113
15. An Incredible Country . . . . . . .123
16. Traveling On . . . . . . . . . . . . . .133

17. Unexpected Events ........................141
18. Our Family Gets Smaller ..................149
19. Making Plans ............................155
20. Going Home .............................163

*Epilogue:* ..............................169
  *The Moores—Beyond Russell Island*
  *Russell Island—Beyond June 1973*

# Meet the Family

DAD rises early to begin his day as a farmer, builder, mechanic, and repairman. He is always on hand to be a Dad to his older sons and a Daddy to the four youngest.

MOM is the organizer, teacher, peacemaker, and record keeper. She designs and sews clothes for the family and keeps everyone on track.

RUSTY, nineteen, has received his Senior Pass (High School diploma) and departed for America to attend college with his stateside friend. With Rusty away, Mickey steps into the role of big brother.

MICKEY, seventeen, is boat skipper, mainland chauffeur, and after-school shopper for home supplies. Mickey's love of architecture and building leads to his best project yet.

Skippy, fifteen, does well with his studies and excels in sports. Always ready for an adventure, Skippy can be counted on to act quickly in an emergency.

Tia, twelve, is capable and reliable. She maintains a happy balance between the three younger ones. Tia loves to cook and is a wonderful help around the house.

Pam, nine, excels as an organizer. She knows where everyone is at a given time. "Curiosity" is her middle name. She is a fund of interesting information.

Jackie, eight, is a redhead like Rusty and her dad. She is thoughtful and considerate. Always looking for someone to help, Jackie makes a friend of every stranger.

Topper, five, loves machines and wants to know how everything works. Like his mother, Topper is always looking for a better way to do things.

*Winter in July—Really!*

# Preface

In this book, I have endeavored to render the truth as accurately as possible. Even though this is my story, it includes many other people who played major or minor roles. In some cases, my interpretation of events will perhaps differ from another's perspective. A few names have been changed because of circumstances.

Dialogue and incidents are reported to the best of my recollection. Although I cannot be certain every quote is entirely accurate word for word, the thoughts, ideas, and circumstances of the story have been preserved.

—Connie Moore

# Prologue

BOOK ONE - *Move to Australia? You've got to be kidding!* The first of this four-book series begins in the early 1960s with the idea of emigrating to Australia. In America, children had rooms full of toys but lacked a sense of responsibility. Captivated by television, they were missing the challenge of outside play. Connie and Bill wanted more traditional values for their family. When Bill retires from the U.S. Navy, the idea becomes reality. With their six children, they sail to the land "down under."

At Sydney, they buy a minivan and head to Western Australia, three thousand miles away. The camping trip, full of adventure, takes them across the desolate, unpaved Nullabor Plain where there are no hotels, motels, or restaurants. A few small towns allow them to stock up on gas and groceries. Traveling back East, they settle in

Brisbane, Queensland—but not for long. Bill discovers the perfect place to raise children. "It's a farm on an island in Redland Bay," he tells Connie. "We can all be farmers."

BOOK TWO - *Me? An Australian Farmer? You've Got to be Kidding!* covers the comedy and pathos of learning to farm in a strange, hemispherically upside-down country. The family copes with a phone service that only operates from 8 a.m. to 8 p.m., a pony who refuses to stay at home, and a farm they nickname *Broken-Downsville*.

In this different world, chickens are *chooks*. Bananas are *trashed*. Shoppers carry their own *tucker* bags. Christmas is celebrated during the heat of summer. And the school year starts in January.

As "farmers-in-training," the family gradually becomes less of a comedy act. They make friends with the islanders and develop new skills. The children excel in their school grades. Broken-Downsville becomes Fiddler's Green, a place of peace and rest. The crops are growing well. The future looks bright. But clouds are gathering on the horizon. The *winds of change* begin to blow across the island.

BOOK THREE - *Sell our Australian Farm? You've Got to be Kidding!* In this book, old friends depart. A bountiful crop creates envy. A new neighbor stirs up anti-Americanism fanned by the Vietnam War. As the weeks pass by, many islanders are turned against them. The Moores grow strong as they learn to cope with adversity. They find creative ways to hold their own. The children are sent to school on the mainland where they make new friends.

Even so, good things do happen. A tennis court, a swimming pool, and the miracle of electric power 24/7. What bliss! Hot water at any time! Dinner at a decent hour. Lights, laundry, all at the flick of a switch!

A new era begins with an imported "grandmother." A son becomes of age and seeks his way in the world. A drought brings planting to a halt. Daily trips to the mainland give island-living a whole different meaning.

*Chapter One*

# Counting Our Blessings

Bill and I sat in the gazebo at Fiddler's Green enjoying our Sunday morning "time off." Mickey was supervising the kitchen cleanup. Skippy was doing outside chores with his little brother, Topper.

I took a sip of coffee and sighed. "Life is a lot different than we expected, isn't it?"

"What do you mean?" Bill asked, sliding over so I could snuggle against him.

"Well, Rusty's in Washington state going to college, and you're working for a land development company at the other end of the island."

"Too right," Bill said. "Boys grow up and leave home, and farmers find other work during drought years. Luckily, I learned to operate heavy equipment as a Navy Seabee. Comes in handy, doesn't it?"

"But what about the farm?" I interrupted. "You put it up for sale without telling me first. I was shocked!"

"I'm sorry," he apologized. "I guess you forgot I had mentioned it on the way home from Rusty's birthday party."

"That was months ago," I protested, moving away from him. "I thought you were kidding."

He reached for my hand. "I was lonely in town all by myself. I missed my family. I began to wonder what the market was for farms on the island. I had no idea the agent would come over to see it without telling me first."

"You're forgiven," I sighed, snuggling close to him again. "It would be wonderful to live on the mainland, but I'd hate to leave our home. We've worked so hard to turn it into a proper country estate—complete with a swimming pool and tennis court."

"You know..." Bill thought for a moment, "when we first came here, the well was full of water. Remember all the rain we had that year?"

"Do I! It rained the day we moved. That's when you discovered the generator had to be cranked. The rain shorted out the electric starter."

Bill chuckled, "What about the stove with a ravenous appetite for wood? We did survive that first day though. Too bad we didn't know how to farm while we still had water. Unfortunately, the well hasn't recovered yet, and I've been told Australia is famous for long droughts."

"Even so, hon, we were lucky to have at least one bumper crop before the drought set in. That one good year, and electricity from the mainland, changed a whole lot of things. We got the house wired and bought a new electric stove and a washing machine. Imagine! Hot water at any time! Dinner at a decent hour! Breakfast toast with an electric toaster! Lights! Laundry! All at the flick of a switch!"

"Don't forget the 1960 station wagon to use on the mainland," Bill reminded me. "Then we bought a blockmaker and cement mixer. They really came in handy. When you sent for them, I had no idea we would be adding a room for my Aunt Jac. Who would have believed that an eighty-three-year-old widow would travel all the way from Maine to Australia? And part of the way by ship."

"She's amazing," I agreed. "Importing Aunt Jac as a grandmother for the children was a special blessing, but there were more blessings to come."

"The swimming pool?" Bill guessed.

"Fair dinkum. The pool, the piano, and one other thing that made a big difference."

"What did I miss?" he scratched his head.

"The *Seagull*," I laughed.

"Of course! How could I forget all the work it took to restore our 20-foot cabin cruiser? Now it looks like new, and we can go to the mainland any time we please. The *Seagull* will work out very well as a school boat too."

"Oh, my goodness," I sat straight up. "School starts again next week! This will be Topper's first year. See… I told you everything is different. How did my baby grow up so fast? I don't think I'm ready for this."

"He'll be fine," Bill comforted.

The following Monday, the children donned their school uniforms. Tia, Pam and Jackie, still in grade school, had yellow plaid dresses with wide-brimmed straw hats. Mickey and Skippy, in high school, wore gray shirts with long pants and *digger* felt hats with wide brims. Topper's first-grade uniform was a gray shirt and shorts with a wide-brimmed cotton sport's hat. The boys carried their books in small, weekend-sized suitcases called *ports*. The girls and Topper had hard-sided backpacks.

*Off to School. Topper peeking out between Jackie and Pam as Mickey loads them on the Ladybug for their ride to the Jetty*

Dressed and ready for the new school year, they clattered happily down the steps. Aunt Jac was at the bottom of the stairs to admire their uniforms and wish them g'day.

"My sakes," she exclaimed when she saw Topper, "you're a big boy now!"

"I have to go," he said heading for the truck. "I don't want to be late for school." Joining him in the truck, we all waved goodbye to Aunt Jac as we headed for the jetty.

Mickey, the *Skipper*, rowed the dinghy out to the *Seagull* anchored off shore. He started the motor and chugged in to the jetty. Bubbling with excitement, the children quickly climbed aboard.

"Be good," I admonished them, with a lump in my throat.

"Yes, ma'am," they promised, waving goodbye as the *Seagull* moved into the channel. With tears misting my eyes, I stood hand-in-hand with Bill, watching the boat disappear around the point.

"They'll be fine," Bill said, reading my thoughts.

"I know, but imagine what a long day this will be for Topper."

"Imagine trying to keep him home," Bill joked.

The day was long. Too long. The house was quiet. Too quiet. Finally, it was time for Bill to pick up the children at the jetty. I busied myself with afternoon snacks, my ears straining for the sound of the Ladybug's return.

When it drove into the yard, I rushed downstairs to hear about their first day at school. At the bottom of the steps, I stopped, bewildered. Bill was alone! The hair on the back of my neck began to prickle.

"What's the matter?" I asked, as my heart skipped a beat.

Trying not to sound worried, he quietly said, "They aren't in yet. Perhaps they couldn't get the engine started."

I knew there was no way I could stay at home and remain calm.

"Hon, why don't we take a ride down to Jacksonville? Perhaps we can see the *Seagull* from there."

We climbed into the truck and drove down to Jacksonville for a better view of the channel. We scanned the horizon but saw no sign of the *Seagull*.

"They may already be home," Bill said, hopefully. "Let's go back."

We drove back to the house. The children weren't there, but the phone was ringing. I ran up the stairs and snatched the receiver.

"Connie here," I answered with as much calm as I could muster.

"This is Mrs. Jackson," a voice said. "Someone just called to tell us that your boat is stalled halfway home. I thought you would like to know."

Melting with relief, I relayed the message to Bill. He reached for the phone and arranged for Mr. Jackson to ferry him out to the *Seagull*. We both agreed not to distress Aunt Jac with the news.

"I'll stay here to fix dinner," I offered. "The kids will be famished by the time they get back to Fiddler's Green."

As Bill headed for the door, I told him to take along some of the bananas hanging under the house for them to snack on.

Dinner was ready by the time I heard the truck motor coming up the road. I ran down the stairs to greet them. Aunt Jac joined me, welcoming them home with open arms. They chatted with her about their first day at school before they rushed upstairs to eat.

I held my questions until they had satisfied their appetites and felt like talking. After a while, Bill began the story.

"When we got there," he said, "the *Seagull* was wallowing in heavy waves. Mr. Jackson told me, 'You go aboard and I'll stand by in case you need help.' He and Mickey steadied the launch for me to climb across to the *Seagull*.

"Once aboard, I looked around and quickly counted noses. I saw Topper sleeping on one of the benches. Because the boat was rocking and pitching, Tia was standing guard to keep him from falling off. Pam and Jackie were leafing through their new school books, happy as larks. Then I realized somebody was missing.

"'Where's Skippy?' I asked.

"'He's out there in the dinghy,' Mickey told me, pointing to a spot between our boat and the Redland Bay jetty...."

At this point, Mickey interrupted his father to explain, "We were out of petrol. Skippy had rowed back to Redland Bay to get some."

Bill nodded and continued, "I hailed Mr. Jackson. He picked me up, and we went into the bay to tow Skippy back with the petrol."

I interrupted with a question I couldn't wait to ask. "How could they run out of petrol? You filled the tank this morning."

Mickey shook his head. "We have no idea. Maybe someone drained the tank just to be mean. You know how it's been lately with all the anti-American stuff."

"What a terrible thing to do!" I exclaimed. "It's hard to believe people could be so spiteful."

"It's not that hard to believe," Skippy said. "Not since Mr. Grosse stirred up some of the islanders to do mean things, just because we're Americans."

Although we had our suspicions, we never did find out who the culprit was. As a precaution, the boys started carrying an extra can of petrol. Fortunately, we had no more trouble with the boat. But this senseless prank added a lot of gray hairs to my collection.

The girls were getting used to their new routine and Topper loved going to school. As parents do, Bill and I hashed over the week during our Sunday gazebo time.

Sipping my coffee, I mused, "At least the girls have settled into the new year at Cleveland Grade School without any problems. Tia told me that all three of them are playing in the Flute Band this year."

"What's a Flute Band?" Bill asked.

"Well, it's a group of flute players. They lead the students during their march to the parade ground for Morning Assembly."

"Is their Morning Assembly anything like mine was in the Navy?"

"There's not a lot difference," I smiled. "While the national anthem is played, they stand on baseball-sized circles in rows. After prayer, the head teacher welcomes them to the school day and makes announcements."

"I hope they don't keel over in the heat," Bill grimaced. "Some sailors used to do that."

"It's hard to believe, but yes they do. It happens in both grade school and high school, according to what Tia and the boys tell me. That's probably the reason wide brimmed hats are a part of the school uniform. Strong English traditions do not always adapt to different climates."

"Mmm," Bill murmured, shifting in his seat, "not like America, is it?"

"Not at all. There are lots of windows in the schools but no screens, no fans, and no electric lights. Australian kids aren't pampered, are they?"

"Well, it doesn't seem to hurt them," Bill shrugged. "They may be less sophisticated than their stateside counterparts, but they're more mature, self-sufficient, and probably happier."

"Too right," I agreed. "The schools may not have a lot of frills, but the grade school has a new pool and swim instructor. The high schoolers use the community pool. Swimming is important in Australia."

Fridays were Sports Days. The children looked forward to Friday after a hard week's work. With lunch over, the entire school changed into gym clothes and participated in a sport of their choice. Those who were exceptionally good, like Skippy, progressed to competitions on the local and state level. In Australia, sports are not the *life* of a school, they're just a wonderful part of it.

All three girls were on swim teams, but Pam was a champion. She was also captain of the fifth grade basketball team. Tia played softball and excelled at track. She and Jackie were star runners.

After a couple of weeks, it became obvious that the school day was too long for Topper. I decided it was best to keep him home when he seemed over-tired. To explain this, I wrote to his teacher using his proper name:

*Dear Miss Guy,*

*We've been anxious to see how the long daily trip would affect Brian. He leaves at seven and doesn't get home until after five. Since he's inclined to be high strung, we must arrange for him to take days off during the first term to unwind and rest.*

> *I'm pleased to note that he is beginning to save things to "show Miss Guy." An indication that he is developing confidence in you. Barring colds, nasty weather, etc., his attendance should become more regular next term. In the meantime, if I can help him along at home please let me know.*

Although it was hard to have the children away for most of the day, we were impressed with the all-round quality of education they were getting.

*Chapter Two*

# Accidents Happen

Although Bill's job with the development company lasted only six months, it gave us a nice cushion to work with. Unfortunately, the drought continued. Bill decided to look for a job on the mainland. Since it was tomato-harvesting season at Redland Bay, he found a job on a farm there and was able to come home each night. Just as the harvest ended, he heard of another developer on Russell Island who needed a grader operator. That was right up his alley. He went to work for Peter Arnold. We were happy to have him working close to home again.

All was well until the Hong Kong Flu swept through our family. Topper, Pam, Jackie, Skippy, and I were all laid up at the same time. In our house, that's very sick. Or "crook" as the Aussies would say. Bill, Mickey, and Tia were the only ones up and moving. Bill went off to work. Mickey and Tia went to school.

One afternoon, when we were all in bed, the phone rang. I waited to see if Skippy would get it. His room was closest.

He struggled out of bed, limped to the phone and answered weakly, "Skippy here." I slid to the edge of my bed, wondering who could be calling. It was Bill. From where I sat, I could hear him shouting over the noise of heavy equipment.

"I've cut my finger," he told Skippy. "I'm going over to the mainland for stitches." I heard the click as he hung up. Something didn't seem quite right to me.

"Is that all he said?" I questioned.

"Yes, ma'am," Skippy assured me. "Then he just hung up."

I struggled out of bed, deciding to be ready for whatever.

"I'm going to take a bath. Let me know if Dad rings again. I want to talk to him."

Late that afternoon, Peter Arnold rang. My hand shook as I held the phone.

"I've just come from Brisbane," he said. "Bill had an accident with a chain saw. He's in the Princess Alexander Hospital. They're working on him right now. At about 6 p.m. you can ring them up to see how he's doing. I'm sorry this happened. I'll stop by tomorrow."

The conversation was over before I could ask all the questions spinning around in my head. Hospital? Doctors? Chain saw? He told Skippy he had cut his finger!

"Mom, was that Dad?" Skippy called.

"No. It was Peter Arnold. He said the doctors are fixing

Dad up. He didn't sound worried. Everything seems to be all right."

That was an exaggeration but there was no use in upsetting the children. They felt bad enough already. I crawled into bed, mentally and physically exhausted.

When Mickey and Tia arrived home, their first question was, "Where's Dad?"

While they fixed dinner for us, I told them what Dad had told Skippy. But I didn't mention the word "chain saw."

"Dad probably won't be home tonight," I explained. "How did things go at school today?" I asked, changing the subject.

Starting at 6 p.m., I called the hospital repeatedly, until the phone service closed down at 8 p.m. It wasn't until the service opened the next morning that I finally connected with a person who could give me some answers. By this time, I was not only sick with the flu, I was close to hysteria.

The doctor wasn't available but a nurse told me, "His arm has been cut in three places. His wrist bone is fractured and a bone in his hand was chipped. I'll have him call you as soon as he is able."

There was nothing else I could do but wait and be thankful that he was still alive.

Peter Arnold came by the next afternoon to check on us and explain the accident.

"Bill was using a chain saw to clear some brush," he said. "When he stepped back, the ground gave away. As he fell, he threw the chain saw away from him. A good move. If it had landed on top of him, no telling what the damage would have been. Unfortunately, it flipped back and cut his arm before it fell to the ground."

Peter expressed his regret and promised to check with us later. I smiled weakly and thanked him for coming.

Mickey, the only one who could get around, went to Brisbane after school to see his dad. They talked about the accident.

"When it happened," his dad told him, "I looked at my arm. Blood was gushing out. I clamped my other hand over it to keep from bleeding to death. I held on during the two hours it took to get to the hospital. Peter Arnold rushed me over to the mainland in his speedboat. An ambulance was waiting at Redland Bay. I kept my hand tight on my arm while they shifted me into the ambulance. I was pretty sure I had cut an artery.

"When they got me to the emergency room, they put me on a table and two doctors came in. One of them said, 'Let me see your arm.' For the first time since the accident, I took my hand off and held out my arm. A stream of blood gushed out. Astonished, the doctor threw up his arms and jumped back. I'll never forget watching the red dots splattering all over his white coat.

"The other doctor got out of the way just in time. 'Looks like a severed artery,' he said. He might have been surprised, but I wasn't. Then everything began to turn foggy. The next thing I remember was looking up at a nurse who was preparing me for surgery. Glancing down, I saw a tourniquet on my arm. They wheeled me into the operating room and stitched everything back together. I don't know how long it took. I was out. When I woke up, the doctor came in and told me my arm would be okay. Tell Mom not to worry, I'll be home soon."

Back at Redland Bay, Mickey missed the ferry hunting for

Tia. She was supposed to be there at the jetty. He called home.

"Mom! I can't find Tia. She wasn't at the jetty when I got there. I went back to her school and checked. She wasn't there either. I don't know what to do and the ferry just left."

"It's all right, Mickey," I calmed him. "Her school bus driver, Mr. Dunn, the one with the abusive tongue, said something that upset her so much she refused to get on the bus. One more smart remark was more than she could cope with. She called to let me know that she's at Ann Marie's house."

"Jolly good," he sighed with relief. "Well, since the ferry has gone, I guess I'll be staying overnight with the Collins. I'll let you know."

"Righto," I replied, relieved that everything was going well on the mainland. Things weren't as well on the island. Our complete work force had been wiped out. I aimed my frustration at the bus company, giving them a blast about Mr. Dunn. They assured me he would be dealt with.

I was ready to drag my weary body back to bed when the phone rang again. It was Tia letting me know that she was all right. Then Mickey rang to tell me he was staying at the Collins. By then the island grapevine kicked in and the phone began to ring every five minutes. It seemed everyone had heard the worst version of Bill's accident. I assured them that he was not going to lose his arm and should be home in a few days.

Thankfully, he was released in just three days. Mickey met him at the jetty and drove him home to Fiddler's Green. He helped him up the stairs and began to fix dinner. The rest of us crawled out of bed to join them.

Dad showed us his arm. It was tinted red, very swollen, and secured in a partial cast and sling.

Wearily he told us, "I got up at dawn to get the bus to Redland Bay for the early boat. I can't talk much now, but I'll tell you all about it tomorrow."

Too exhausted to eat, he joined the rest of us in our misery. The little ones were much improved, but Skip and I were still crook.

Two weeks passed, most of it spent in bed. Oddly, it turned out to be one of the finest vacations we've ever had. Whoever felt best got up, did a bit of work, and crawled back into bed. I was in charge of entertainment. On the weekends, I read to Bill and Tia by the hour. In between, I read different stories to the smaller ones. Sometimes we had so many people in our bed, I was afraid it would collapse.

It almost did the day Mickey handed me an airmail letter from Rusty. Everyone scurried into our room, and perched on the bed to hear what their big brother was doing.

"Guess what!" I said, scanning the letter. "Your brother is in the Army! Oh, my gosh! I wonder how that happened so fast."

I read on. "He says he did very well on his mid-term exams—just a whisker away from a 3.0 average. Jolly good! Considering he transferred from the British system to the American system, I think he did very well."

"He certainly did!" Bill said proudly.

I read on. "Earlier this year, I went home with my roommate for a visit. His father took me up in their Piper Cub twice during the weekend. I even got a chance to take the controls. I loved the feeling of soaring high above the ground...."

"That's just like Rusty," Skippy broke in. We all nodded in agreement.

"What's a Piper Cub?" Topper wanted to know.

"It's a small propeller plane," Skippy explained.

I continued. "After final exams, I planned a trip to visit our relatives. When I found out how close to the top my draft number was, I canceled the trip at the last minute. I needed at least a year at university to get into Naval Pilot's School. Afraid I'd be stuck on the ground, I joined the army. After basic, I'll go to Fort Walters, Texas, to train as a helicopter pilot."

"What's a helicopter pilot?" Topper interrupted again.

"I'll tell you in a minute," Pam hushed him. "What else did he say, Mom?"

"He finished his letter asking about everyone. He wants to know what you're doing in school and how things are on the island. He's also concerned about Dad's arm and Aunt Jac."

"Is that all?" Jackie asked when I paused.

"Yes. If you'll pass me my tablet and pen, I'll answer the letter."

"Come on," Pam took Topper's hand. "Now, I can tell you about helicopter pilots."

As the children drifted off, I propped myself up against the pillows and began to write:

Dear Rusty,

> Things have settled down on the island since Dad went to the Minister of Education. Someone at the top must have had a little talk with Mr. Grosse.
>
> Mickey will sit for Senior next year. If he makes the grade he'll go on to teacher's college. Skippy has just finished his Junior Public Exams. Whether good or bad he'll continue on to Senior. Usually he does very well on test scores so we're not worried. When Dad was working, he and

*Mickey did all the muscle work on the farm.*

*The girls are taking over more chores in the house and kitchen. They do all the things you boys used to do at that age. We even have a chart for them to keep track of their jobs. When they earn money they jot it down in the little notebook like you did. I'm sure there was a time when you thought they would never be required to do your jobs, but everyone grows up eventually.*

*Topper is a good all rounder. He's still working out the best way to do things. He would rather mow the lawn than empty wastebaskets. He considers that a baby job. He's right, but what do you do when there are no more babies? Tia and I have no one to hold and pet.*

*Aunt Jac is getting along well. She feels more at home with the change of seasons than she did last year, and she is raising some beautiful zinnias in the front garden. She tells stories to the girls and pays Pam a dime to clean her room and do errands.*

*Dad's arm is healing well. I try to stay close and supply an extra arm when he needs it, to save him from over-using his. Peter Arnold has been by a few times to see how he is getting on. He should be able to go back to work soon.*

*Congratulations on doing so well on your exams. You always were smarter than you gave yourself credit for. I know you'll do a great job in the army too. We're proud of you and we all miss you. Take care of yourself and write soon.*

*Love and Blessings*

Although we didn't want to talk about it, Bill and I knew it was a sure, short trip from helicopter school to war in Vietnam.

*Rusty the helicopter pilot.*

*Chapter Three*

# We Go By Boat

"The circus is going to be at Redland Bay!" the kids squealed as they ran up the stairs with their school ports. "Can we go? Can we go?"

I looked at Bill. His wounds were healing, but the wrist bone fracture and the chipped bone in his hand kept him grounded. The doctor told us it would be quite a while before his arm was completely mobile again.

Sensing my thoughts, Bill said, "You go with the kids. I'll be all right. We've always wanted to take them to a circus and with Redland Bay so close, it would be a shame to miss it."

"Goodie, goodie," Pam and Jackie sang as they danced in a circle together.

"Righto," Tia said. "You can come over on the afternoon ferry and ride back with us on the *Seagull*."

"Jolly good," I approved. "We could eat somewhere before the circus."

Skippy begged off. "Can I stay the night with a friend? I've been to a circus before. I'd like to go home from school with Kevin."

"Fine, but first you'll need his mother's permission."

With everything decided, my stomach began to churn. The prospect of a trip across the water in a small boat always affects me that way. *I have to get over this,* I prayed.

From the back of my mind, I recalled a Bible verse we had just read: "Ask and ye shall receive." I asked for peace and freedom from the fear of small boats.

*If that word is true,* I told myself, *then there's nothing more to worry about.*

The day of the circus, I permed my hair and finished the boleros that matched the girl's new skirts. I tucked their outfits into my basket with a change of clothes for Topper. We were entering the spring rainy season. The days could be hot and dry or chilly and damp. As I drove down to the jetty, I realized we were going to crop a bit of weather.

The trip over on the afternoon launch was rough, much worse than usual. As the ferry skipper struggled to tie up at Redland Bay, I watched our *Seagull* wildly gyrating at anchor. *If the sea is this rough on a big ferry,* I thought, *how will we manage to get home in our much smaller* Seagull?"

I went up on deck to wait my turn to debark. There was no ramp from boat to jetty. Usually it was one simple step up or down, depending on the tide. But not today. I watched as the passengers very carefully timed their step from the heaving boat to the jetty. One slip could, and sometimes did, result in a broken arm or leg.

I moved up to the rail just as a great gust of wind blew across the bay. Before I could blink, the top of my basket blew open. Out flew my book, wallet, and the girls' boleros. They splashed into the water. Too close to the rocks for the launch to reach and too far away to be snagged by a boat hook.

"Oh, no," I moaned. "There goes the circus and our dinner money."

Mickey, who had just arrived in the station wagon, jumped out and ran along the jetty. He climbed aboard the launch.

"Mr. Noyes, can you take me in a little closer?"

"Yes," he nodded, and inched his way into the bay as far as he could.

Mickey quickly pulled off his watch, shoes, and shirt and dived into the water.

"Superman to the rescue," I wanted to shout.

Everything had miraculously floated. He scooped them up, waded ashore and rushed up to the car.

By the time the ferry inched its way back to the jetty, Mickey had changed into his dry sports uniform. Like superman, he just happened to have a change of clothes on hand. And he didn't even need a phone booth. I laughed at the silly thought, relieved and pleased.

Meeting him coming down the jetty, I praised him. "You saved the day, Mickey!"

He beamed. "It was fun," he said.

On the way up from the jetty, Jackie pointed excitedly. It was the circus tent. We could see it being raised in an empty field. It would have been fun to watch it go up, but Topper brought us back to reality.

"I'm hungry," he pleaded, tugging on my sleeve.

Tia interceded on a practical note. "We need to go eat so we can come back in time to watch the circus."

With that good advice, we piled into the car and drove to the community pool lunchroom for hamburgers.

"Sorry," they told us, "the lunchroom is only open on weekends."

While we were deciding what to do next, Topper forgot about being hungry. He had spotted one of his friends in the pool.

"Mom, Mom, can I go swimming?" I looked at the girls and Mickey. They nodded.

"Can I?" Topper asked again.

I smiled down at him. "Luckily, I packed a change of clothes for you so it's all right to get wet. Yes, you can go swimming."

Mickey decided to give it a go too. After all, how much wetter can you get than wet? The girls and I, huddled in a sheltered corner, watched them swim.

Just short of starvation, we got Topper out and changed him into dry clothes. Mickey borrowed a towel, wrung himself out thoroughly, and re-donned his wet shorts.

"There's a snack bar in Cleveland," he said. "If we hurry it may still be open."

We took a chance and got there just in time to enjoy hamburgers and crisps. Warm, fed, and almost dry, we headed back to Redland Bay for the circus.

"Where's the tent?" Tia asked as we topped the hill.

"Oh, no," Pam sighed, "it's not up yet." The tent was almost flat.

As we watched, a gust of wind tumbled it to the ground. We got out of the car and went to ask if there was any hope.

"I'm sorry," a burly man in shirtsleeves apologized, "it's too windy to raise the big top. The circus is canceled."

I was wondering how to deal with the disappointment when Topper and Pam came running up.

"Mama, Mama, come and see!" they shouted. We followed them around the tent to a grassy field where camels, horses, and elephants were munching on grass. Monkeys on leashes were running to and fro.

"Fair dinkum," I said in surprise. "Usually we see circus animals performing in a tent or pacing in cages for people to stare at. It isn't often you get to see them just being natural." We may have missed the Big Top but we certainly enjoyed the show in front of us.

"Want to go visit my friend Ian?" Mickey asked, when the kids were ready to move on.

"What would his mother think of our whole family showing up without notice?" I scolded. "That wouldn't be very polite."

"He's expecting us," Mickey insisted. "I told him we might come by later. I told Dad, too, so he won't be wondering where we are."

Proud of him for having done the proper thing and letting his dad know the situation, I readily agreed to the visit.

When we arrived at Ian's, he apologized that his mother could not be there.

"She really wanted to meet you and asked me to put the teapot on for a cup of tea," he said ushering us into the parlor.

We sipped tea and visited until the wind calmed down and the tide had reached its lowest ebb. With heartfelt thanks for the tea and biscuits, we said "tata" and headed for the jetty.

Tia and the small ones settled in the boat cabin. Mickey and I peered through the windscreen into the black sea spray. It was misty and pitch dark. We strained to see but couldn't find the yellow buoys that marked the safe travel lane.

Trying to work our way over into the lea of Garden Island, we slowed until we were wallowing in the waves. Suddenly, Mickey spotted a beacon just in front of us.

"There's one!" he yelled. "Funny, I didn't see a beacon there this morning."

"When I came over, I didn't see it either. I bet an angel put it there just for us. We are blessed."

Dripping wet and shivering with cold we found the other markers and thankfully pulled into our jetty.

Low tide at Russell Island is no joke. The wharf is six feet up and the boat is six feet down. The ladder that bridges the gap had rotted off at the high water mark. All of our passengers were asleep. We were able to rouse the girls, slightly.

"Hang on to something," I shouted, while I pulled from above and Mickey pushed from below.

Topper could not be roused at all. "Topper, reach your hand up!" I demanded in a stern voice.

"Topper, stand on this," Mickey insisted. But Topper slept blissfully on— unaware that he was tottering inches from a cold dip in the bay or a warm bed at home. It could go either way.

Finally, in desperation, Mickey scooped him up, threw him over his shoulder, and climbed up the ladder. Our hero had triumphed again!

"Oh, the joys of island living," I sighed. Suddenly, I realized that I had not been afraid during the entire trip. God's Word is true! I felt like Pam and Jackie when they danced around singing "goodie, goodie."

*Chapter Four*

# Oh No, Not Again!

Our circus caper blissfully faded from my mind until the next big event at school. The day of the Fancy Dress Ball left me asking myself, *Do I really want to live on an island? Maybe Bill has the right idea about selling the farm and moving to the mainland.*

A cousin to America's Halloween costume parties, the November Fancy Dress Ball is one of the biggest events of the year. Once again, we would be crossing the water and possibly get rained out. The sky held no promise of sun. It drizzled all day.

When the kids came home from school, I was certain they were going to tell me the Ball had been cancelled. But they didn't. I called the school to make sure. It would have been a shame to waste the costumes but it was so wet and windy.

"No," was the answer, "it's still on."

I looked at the children. "You don't really want to go back over there in such bad weather, do you?"

"Yes, yes," they pleaded in unison, sealing our fate.

Topper, the practical one, suggested, "We can take an umbrella."

"As well as raincoats and boots," I joked. We packed up and began the usual load-unload sequence. On to the truck, off the truck, on to the jetty trolley, off the jetty trolley, and on to the boat. The same sequence was reversed when we reached Redland Bay. Oh, the joys of island living!

Skippy had stayed on the mainland with a friend, but Mickey and Bill were both on board to manage the boat. I let them peer through the mist to watch for beacons while I took care of more important things. For days, the girls had talked about creating exotic hairdo's for the grand occasion. They gave directions as I combed, pinned, and braided. In no time, it seemed, we were at Redland Bay. I still had one more head of hair to do.

"What about me?" Pam cried.

"I'll do it in the car," I promised.

Bill inched in to the jetty using his one good arm. Mickey jumped across to tie up. He handed us on to the jetty with all our gear.

"I'll get the boat anchored and row in," he told his dad.

"Jolly good, Mickey. I'll walk up to the parking lot for the car."

"Will you be able to drive?" Mickey worried.

"I've still got one good arm," Dad grinned.

I could see that Topper was getting tired. I encouraged him to ride on the trolley while the girls pushed. By the time we reached the end of the jetty, Mickey was rowing in to the beach. He tied up the dinghy and joined us to wait for Dad.

"What took so long to anchor the *Seagull*?" I asked.

"Well," he sighed, "I wanted to be sure it could cope with the wind, waves, tide, drift, and everything else I could think of." He finished with a wry grin, "We sure don't want to find the boat at the bottom of the bay when we come back this year."

"Goodness, no," I agreed. I really didn't want to be reminded of the storm that had sunk the *Seagull* during last year's Fancy Dress Ball. As if on cue, to save me from that memory, Dad arrived with the car.

We all piled aboard and headed for the school. Sitting in the back seat, I worked on Pam's hair.

"We're going to be late," she moaned, twisting to look out the window.

"Hold still and let me finish! When we get there, you and Jackie only have to slip into your long skirts and bonnets. You'll look just like proper old fashioned girls."

"All I need to do is put on my cowboy hat," Topper said, confident that he had everything under control.

Skippy was waiting for us at the school.

"It's almost time for the Grand March," he warned. "Hurry, get your costumes on."

I helped the girls into their skirts and tied their sashes and bonnet ribbons. I turned around to check on Tia. She was just standing there, with a look of dismay on her face. Inspired by Aunt Jac, she had chosen to wear an Indian sari. Aunt Jac had carefully instructed her on how to drape the long piece of silk. She had practiced for days. But now, in a moment of panic, she forgot.

"I can't do it," she wailed.

I reminded her that it was Aunt Jac who had taught her, not me. I looked her in the eye and calmed her down with a few stiff words. "I can't help you. You did it at home. You can do it now. Get busy." I don't suppose any sari was ever wrapped with the speed of that one. She was gracefully draping the loose end over her head and shoulder as she stepped into place for the Grand March. When the line began to move, she looked back at me and grinned.

The Grand March was a huge success. I was proud of the Moore kids. They had chosen well. After it was over and the program progressed, the mist became heavier. Finally, in the middle of the puppet show, it began to rain.

"The Fancy Dress Ball," it was announced over the loud speaker, "has been regretfully concluded."

Mickey found us as we were preparing to leave.

"Mr. and Mrs. Cooper are here and would like to meet you," he said. "They're the people who live just across from the school. I visit them a lot. Their oldest boy, Clive, is in my grade and his brother, Stuart, is in Skippy's grade."

We walked over to say g'day and were invited to come to their house for a cuppa.

"It would be pretty wet going back to the bay right now," Mr. Cooper reasoned. "Perhaps the storm will pass by while you're having tea with us."

We accepted the invitation and promised to walk over as soon as we rounded up the children. I was especially comfortable with the idea of waiting for a break in the weather. Cruising through a storm was not on my list of fun things to do.

We collected the children, who were moaning about the ball being rained out. They quickly perked up when we told them where we were going. We walked across the street and were comfortably settled in the Cooper's living room, while Mrs. Cooper busied herself preparing tea.

Not able to relax, I perched on the edge of the sofa. "What's the use of having a boat to go back and forth in, if the weather won't cooperate?" I complained.

"It was fun just the same." Tia smiled, trying to cheer me up.

"And we did get to do the Grand March," Pam said, prancing across the room.

Jackie knelt on the floor beside me. She put her elbows on my lap and looked up at me. Her freckled face was solemn, her blue eyes serious.

"I had fun," she pleaded. "Can we do it again next year?"

"Hey, what's a little rain?" Skippy clowned. "We won't melt, will we? Besides, it's nice to be here with Mr. and Mrs. Cooper. And maybe next year, the school will build a big hall so we can have our events inside."

We all laughed at that improbability.

Mrs. Cooper poured a round of tea. Tensions released, I smiled and melted into the comfortable sofa beside Bill. Sipping my tea, I thought of how easy it was to live on the mainland. Maybe someday, I thought.

As we were getting ready to leave, Mrs. Cooper asked if I would be interested in helping at the high school Tuck Shop during the next school year.

"The Tuck Shop?" I asked.

"Yes, it's run by the Parents and Citizens Organization. Since there is no cafeteria at the school, we provide food for the children to purchase at recess and lunchtime. We stock drinks, meat pies, sausage rolls, biscuits, and crisps."

"I know what crisps are," Topper piped up. "They're potato chips."

"You're right." Mrs. Cooper smiled down at him.

"I don't know much about Tuck Shops," I hesitated. "What would I be doing?"

"The mothers volunteer to make sandwiches and serve the children while the Tuck Shop is open. You would only be scheduled for one day each month."

I thanked her for asking and said I'd talk it over with Bill. I was excited at the prospect of seeing an Australian school in operation.

On the way home—over much smoother waters—Bill and I, standing watch on the deck, talked about the Tuck Shop.

"Do you think it would be a good idea?" I asked.

"Well, all the children are in school and there's not much going on with the farm. Why not give it a go?" was his opinion.

*Chapter Five*

# Learning to Cope

Bill and I sat in the gazebo with our Sunday morning coffee. We talked about how well the children were managing with the *Seagull* as their school boat.

"I have a thought," I said, looking dreamily at the sky.

Bill tensed. When your wife has a "thought," it's almost as serious as when she says "hon."

"Tell me about it," he said warily.

"Well, if we're going to be traveling to the mainland for school activities, wouldn't it be better to have a faster boat?"

Bill relaxed. "I like your thought. How about a jet boat? It's a new concept here. They're supposed to be as fast as a speedboat, but they have an inboard motor. That would save us from carrying an outboard motor back and forth to the jetty."

Pleased that we agreed, Bill made

arrangements with a boat builder near Wellington Point to build us a jet boat. After three long months, lots of phone calls, and mountains of frustration, the boat still wasn't ready. There was always another excuse.

"I just called about the boat," Bill said, hanging up the phone one day. "It's almost ready but it still needs to be painted inside."

"How long will that take?" I asked.

"They weren't able to give me a date," he frowned. I knew he was angry.

"Couldn't we take delivery now and paint it ourselves?" I suggested.

"Jolly good," he brightened, "let's give it a go!"

The boat arrived within a few days. It was a sleek 16-footer made of wood. The spacious cabin was outfitted with comfortable benches and a sleeping area. We painted it royal blue, with a white cabin and white trim.

"Looks better than anything on the bay," I boasted, as we admired our work.

"Too right," Bill said, "and just in time for Speech Night."

Like American graduation events, Speech Night celebrates the end of Queensland's school year. The mayor and school dignitaries are invited to make speeches. The Principal gives a report on the year's events and recognizes students for their achievements. Skippy was scheduled to receive an award for excelling in hurdles and high jump competitions—an event we didn't want to miss.

Bill attached all the fixtures to the boat and pronounced it ready. We called a family council to decide on a name for our new boat.

## Learning to Cope

After a number of improbable suggestions, I asked, "What flies faster than a seagull?"

"An eagle!" Topper shouted.

"We can call it the *Eagle*," Tia said, "because it will zoom faster than the *Seagull*."

"A lot faster," Mickey corrected. "With the jet boat, we can make the forty-five minute trip to the mainland in fifteen minutes. But it takes another fifteen minutes to unload and tie up."

"Mooring a boat is getting to be quite an art," Skippy added dolefully. "Especially since they built the new Redland Bay jetty."

"Why's that?" I asked.

"It's the cement steps down each side," he explained. "They're supposed to make it easier for people to get off and on the boats. But they make it a lot harder to tie the boats up."

Mickey agreed, "It's a proper dingo (that's Aussie for *not good*). When the seas are up, the skippers are always complaining about their boats taking a beating from the cement steps. That jetty was obviously designed by someone who had never docked a boat in rough weather."

It was that kind of weather that greeted us when we crossed on Speech Night. Because Bill's arm was still healing, Mickey piloted the boat. Maneuvering a jet was a new experience for him, and this was not the best weather for a novice.

Mooring was as bad as Skippy had predicted. It was so turbulent, the boat smashed into the jetty and broke a bit off the corner of the cabin roof. Mickey was crushed.

"She'll be all right," Dad reassured him. "You and I can fix that later."

We arrived early and were able to find good seats for the outdoor event. It was late November, summer had just begun. The wind, so frustrating on the bay, was more than welcomed on the hot parade ground.

Occasionally, dark clouds rumbled above us, but the rain held off. It was a great evening and the speeches were good. Skippy proudly received the award for his athletic performance during the year. After the festivities and congratulations, a tired but happy group headed home to Fiddler's Green.

The trip back was uneventful, but the next day found most of us in bed with no energy to move. The little ones, who had slept on the way home, were up bright and early reading books. Mickey and Skippy were snug in bed, sleeping as only teenagers can. They were blissfully confident that the world was capable of spinning without their help.

"One of us has got to get up and feed the children," I groaned.

"They seem to be doing fine without us," Bill mumbled into his pillow. "They'll let us know when we're needed." I decided he was right. A cozy bed is a perfect place on a rainy day.

The little ones found things to keep them occupied. Later Mickey served us coffee and cooked a late breakfast for everyone. In the afternoon, between naps, I read a mystery story to Bill and Tia.

Days of quiet peacefulness, without a list of "must-be-done's," are so rare, I hoard them in my memory bank like jewels in a vault. I savor every moment. Tomorrow hovers just around the corner, and who knows what that will bring. Too quickly, life returned to normal.

Before his accident, Bill and I had arranged to take a series of guitar lessons over at Cleveland, on the mainland. Since he was getting better, we decided to give it a go. We gathered the things we needed to take: guitar, clothes, shoes, torch (flashlight), and extra petrol. We left at 6:30 p.m. to be sure we got there by eight o'clock. I drove the truck down to the jetty.

We loaded the trolley from the truck, pushed it to the end of the jetty, and loaded everything into the dinghy. Bill got in, and I rowed out to the boat. At this stage, I was still doing all the rowing. Unfortunately, I don't have his muscles, so it took longer to get there. We boarded the boat. I hauled in the big anchor and Bill started the motor. I sat back, pleased because we had done so well. We were off to another grand adventure.

"Oh no!" I wailed, jumping up.

"What's the matter?" Bill jerked his head around in alarm.

"I forgot my clothes. I left them hanging on the door. I can't possibly arrive there in khaki work clothes." Without a word, he turned the boat. It took several passes with his one-arm driving to get in to the jetty.

I dashed home in the truck, snatched my clothes and raced back. By then it was pitch dark, and our searchlights wouldn't work—but do they ever when we need them? We spent ages hunting for beacons, and had difficulty mooring the boat at Redland Bay.

"We're going to be late," I wailed, as we finally climbed on to the jetty. It was eight o'clock, and I was feeling like a frustrated tiger. Grabbing the guitar, we rushed to the parking lot and climbed into the car. I waited for Bill to start the motor. Instead, he opened the door and got out.

I leaned over. "What's the matter?"

"Mickey gave me the wrong key," he mumbled. It took more precious minutes to find the spare. Finally, we were on the road. My unaccepted apologies were still hanging in the air, when suddenly Bill began to stomp on the floorboard.

"The dimmer switch isn't working," he fumed. "I can't make the lights bright."

Sliding down in my seat, I murmured to myself, "There's nothing quite like living on an island and zipping over to the mainland for an evening's outing."

The lesson was half over by the time we arrived. We apologized to the teacher and pretended we knew what he was talking about as the lesson progressed.

Although the following week's crossing was dark, rainy, and rough, we managed to be on time for the lesson. I spent most of the trip praying that I'd learn to love this sort of life.

Going home was dreadful. I stood watching the water and clutching the cabin roof. If the boat was going to tip over, I was determined I'd be on my feet when it did. We pitched and rolled all the way to the lea of Garden Island. Out of the wind, the boat finally settled down.

The next day, when Bill came home from taking care of the *Eagle*, he was puzzled.

"I wonder where the scratches on the cabin roof came from. They weren't there the other day."

I didn't offer an explanation, but I had an idea they were made by my fingernails. During our trip home, I had been hanging on to the roof to keep my rubbery knees from collapsing.

## Learning to Cope

That Sunday, in the gazebo, I made a casual observation. "Instead of going all the way across the bay, I think we could learn just as much from a beginner's book right here at home."

Bill didn't comment, but a look of relief flashed across his face. Smiling, he changed the subject.

"Friday I have to go to Brisbane. I have an appointment with the doctor there to check my arm."

Bill was jubilant when he came home. "The doctor gave me clearance to go back to work," he announced. "I'll go down tomorrow to tell Peter Arnold the good news."

When he got there, Peter was packing up his equipment and getting ready to leave.

"Sorry, mate," he said with sincerity, "but we've finished here." It was disappointing. But we were thankful that when he was working, we had been able to set aside money for just such an emergency.

There were no other jobs on the island. Rather than do nothing, Bill decided to try for something in Brisbane. It wasn't long before he was hired by Arnotts Biscuit Company to be trained as a mechanic.

The kids were sorry he would only be home on weekends, but they were thrilled about his working for a biscuit company. (Aussies call cookies *biscuits*). As he boarded the ferry with his suitcase, Topper made one last request.

"Can you bring home some of those bickies when you come?" he asked.

Bill smiled and waved, "I'll see what I can do," he promised.

Later he called to tell us he had found a comfortable room in Mrs. Green's boarding house. "She's very nice, like a mother," he reported.

*Chapter Six*

# Adventures in the Big City

The excitement of School Break-Up and Christmas was over. We had hit the doldrums of summer vacation.

"What can we do?" Tia moaned. "There's nothing to do on the farm. The boys are away and Dad isn't here. We don't have anything to do. Can't we go somewhere?"

"I want to go see Daddy," Pam pleaded.

"I wish you could, but Dad's working."

Jackie put in her bid, "Everyone goes away in the summer," she reasoned. "Why can't we?"

"We really do need to do something different," I admitted. "Let me think about it for a while."

When Bill rang that evening, I told him about our problem.

"Your children are bored and they miss their daddy. They want to go somewhere. Any suggestions?"

"Hmm," he mused. "Perhaps you and the kids could come over and stay with me for a week. I don't think Mrs. Green would mind. I'll ask her and ring you back."

Mrs. Green gave her approval, and Bill booked an extra room so we wouldn't be crowded.

In the morning, I announced the good news to the children. After they finished jumping up and down with excitement, we began to make plans for a week's stay in the big city of Brisbane.

"City Hall first," Jackie said. "My teacher told us the tower is as high as a twenty-story building. I want to climb up there."

"That's right," Tia agreed. Then, drawing from her seventh grade information pool, she added, "For years and years it was the only tall building in Brisbane. Taking the stairs up to the top of the tower has always been a special thing to do. From there, you can see all around the city."

"Sounds good to me," I said, jotting down *Number One: City Hall Tower*. "By the way, Dad told me he can arrange for a tour of the factory where he works. They'll show us how cookies, or rather biscuits, are made. They pass out samples too. That can be Number Two."

Topper was suddenly interested in our planning session. "You mean we can have some bickies?" he grinned. I nodded.

"Can we go to the pineapple factory after that?" Pam asked. "The island school went there once. Our grade wasn't old enough to go. That could be Number Three."

"Do we get to eat pineapples too?" I could tell Topper was getting hungry.

"We'll know when we get there," Jackie said, giving him a hug.

Always ready to organize, Pam stood up. "Let's get busy and pack," she suggested.

The vacation was a great experience. The children were thrilled to see Daddy at work in the biscuit factory. They felt like royalty when he gave them crunchy chocolate chip cookies right off the assembly line.

The pineapple factory was another fun trip. At the end of the tour, we were treated to sweet pieces of pineapple and freshly pressed juice in tiny cups. Pam fell in love with the pineapple juice fountain. She kept returning with her little cup.

"Just one more little cupful," she pleaded, when I announced it was time to go.

Another day, we took a picnic lunch to the new downtown plaza in front of City Hall. While we ate, a flock of pigeons kept us entertained. Bustling around pecking at crumbs, they stopped only long enough to cock an eye at us as if to say, *Where's your contribution?* We scattered our sandwich scraps and watched them squabble over them.

"That's our contribution!" Jackie proclaimed with satisfaction, before we drifted off.

Cole's Department Store was our next big adventure. We planned to explore the whole store and finish with dinner in the cafeteria. The smaller children had never experienced a cafeteria—or a five-story department store. We browsed through furniture, luggage, and kitchen appliances.

"We already have enough of those," Tia complained, hoping to move on to something more interesting.

"What's Haber... Haberdashery? Do we need one of those?" Pam asked, reading a sign.

"No, that's the men's clothing department. Let's go look at the fabrics. They might have some pretty materials for new dresses."

"What about fish and chips?" Topper questioned. Obviously, he was not interested in choosing dress materials.

"That's right," Jackie piped up. "You said we could go up to the cafeteria on the fifth floor. Can we ride the elevator?"

I looked at my watch. It agreed with Topper's stomach. We found the elevator and soared up to the fifth floor.

"That tickles my tummy," Jackie giggled. Life was full of new experiences. I don't know which they enjoyed most, the elevator or the fish and chips.

The next day, we climbed aboard an old-fashioned electric tram to explore the city. We were getting tired of just looking when I noticed the Ice Cream Shoppe. I rang the bell to stop the tram. The children all wanted to know what we were stopping for.

"You'll see in just a minute," I promised.

After I paid our fares, we walked back to the Ice Cream Shoppe for double-decker ice cream cones. This was not a common event for island children. Their biggest quandary was trying to decide which flavor should go on top and what would taste best on the bottom.

"Have your favorite put on the bottom," big sister Tia advised, "that way you'll have the best taste last."

We sat on a bench in the shade to enjoy our treat.

"What's next?" Pam asked, lapping the drips on the side of her cone.

"I thought it would be fun to take a tram to the theater to see what's playing." Before I finished talking, they were up and ready to go.

## Adventures in the Big City

When the tram stopped, Jackie was the first one off.

"Look, Mom," she pointed to the marquee, "It's the *Sound of Music!* All my friends have been talking about this movie! Can we go see it? Pretty please?" she coaxed. The movie was the perfect climax to our wonderful week of exciting events in the big city. I heard "doe, a deer, a female deer..." all through the house for weeks.

At home, we realized that Aunt Jac had enjoyed our vacation too. With school out, having four young children around all day, every day, was a bit much for her. A lot of extra movement and a lot of extra noise. Fortunately, she had developed a circle of friends who kept her busy. When she needed to get away, they were always glad to see her. For longer breaks, she and seventy-year-old Miss Watts, who lived just down the road, would go "walkabout."

"What's that?" she asked the first time Miss Watts invited her to go walkabout.

"That's what the aborigines do," Miss Watts explained. "When the spirit moves them, they pack up all their belongings and walk out into the desert. It's pretty hard on the station owners though. They never know when, or how long, their work force will be away. Time means nothing to aborigines on a walkabout."

"Oh, I see," Aunt Jac chuckled. She was delighted with the idea of acting like an aborigine.

She and Miss Watts formed a habit of taking long walks around the island. When they came to an interesting spot, they stopped to have a cuppa.

One day, Aunt Jac told me, "Miss Watts always carries a 'billy' to boil water for tea." She looked at me solemnly.

"Did you know that a billy is only a tin can with a bit of wire for a handle?"

She was amazed when Miss Watts introduced her to the art of making a "tiny" fire. Demonstrating, Miss Watts made a little pile of dry grass and twigs. "Not big enough to start a bush fire," she cautioned her, "just big enough to boil the billy. The grass is to start the fire, and the twigs supply the heat to boil the water."

She also shared her incredible knowledge of the flora and fauna of Australia, a subject dear to Aunt Jac's heart. She loved to learn how things were done in different countries. We were delighted with the interesting bits of information she brought home and pleased to know she was getting along so well.

During our chats, she often told me about a story she had read when she lived in England. It was about a European grandmother.

"The grandmother was held in high esteem," she reminisced with a dreamy smile. "In the evenings, she sat in a lovely royal chair. It was on a little dais. All the children used to come and kneel before her to hear her words of wisdom."

After a few repetitions of this story, I began to think, *Am I missing something? Are we supposed to be training our children to treat her like a royal matriarch? But—wait a minute. Just what did that queenly grandmother do to deserve such attention? How many children did she raise to get all that wisdom?*

One day, sitting over cups of coffee, we began to talk about raising children. It was obvious that she was quite out of touch with the subject. I didn't want to pry, but I had to know.

I timidly asked, "Why didn't you have any children, Aunt Jac? Was it because you weren't able to?"

"Goodness no," was her quick answer. "I didn't want any."

*Oh, dear*, I thought, *I hope Aunt Jac isn't on a collision course with reality.*

*Chapter Seven*

# New Horizons

Life was beginning to settle into a fairly comfortable routine. Although Bill was gone during the week, he was home to spend time with the children on the weekends. Mickey had a summer job on the mainland and Skippy, our "hired hand," took care of what needed to be done on the farm.

Sunday mornings were still special. We had our little "church time" followed by Bill's famous pancakes and my award-winning fruit compote. After breakfast, carrying fresh cups of coffee, we retired to the gazebo while the children did the kitchen chores.

"What have you got planned for today?" was Bill's first question.

"Glad you asked. Do you realize that ever since we've been here, I've been busy with the farm, the house, and the children? I don't know anything about the rest of the island."

"Not quite true," he joked. "You must be very familiar with the road between here and the jetty."

I jabbed him in the ribs with my elbow.

"Ouch," he laughed.

"Well, you deserved it. Next, I suppose you'll be telling me I should know all about Canipia road, just because we walk down there to see Ron and Jack in the evenings. You know perfectly well it's too dark to see anything," I huffed.

"Okay, I give up. What are you trying to tell me?"

"I think it's time to broaden my horizons."

"What do you mean? You want to take a trip to Europe?"

"No, silly! I want to explore the island."

He straightened up, ready for action. "Where do you want to go first?"

"Let's explore the other end of the island where they've been doing all the clearing. We can take Topper, the girls, and a picnic lunch."

The children loved the idea. When we visited places they had already seen, they pointed out landmarks and told stories of their adventures there. Our Sunday excursions with Daddy were the high spots of summer vacation. Until, too quickly, it was time for another school year.

After the children settled into their new routine, I called Mrs. Cooper and asked to be signed up for duty in the Tuck Shop. My horizons were expanding again. With no children at home, I could do things on the mainland. When my Thursday turn came around, I traveled over on the *Eagle* with the kids. Mickey, our mainland chauffeur, drove us to school and directed me to the Tuck Shop.

I introduced myself and explained my lack of knowledge. The three co-workers, lovely ladies, took me under their wings. They patiently introduced me to meat pies, sausage rolls, and soft drinks (Australian for soda pop).

While we sliced buns and chopped lettuce together, I learned more about Australia, and they learned more about America. I was impressed by their "mother network." They swapped needs, and solved each other's problems. Like finding the right job—or mate, for their children. They knew who was sick and what to do for them. They knew where to get things taken care of, and who was best qualified to do the job.

The Tuck Shop gave me a whole new, refreshing look at Australia. No problem was too big for the Tuck Shop ladies to solve. With their acceptance and care, I began to feel closer to becoming a part of this amazing country.

In March, Curtis Routledge rang up Bill. "Thought you'd like to know," he drawled, "there's a job opening over here on 'Straddie.' They need another dredge operator. It's good pay. You'll have to come to Straddie and apply at the office in Dunwich." They chatted for a while about the job, the farm, and the island.

Hanging up the phone, Bill asked, "What do you think of my working over on Stradbroke Island?"

"What would you be doing?"

"I'd be operating a barge for a sand mining company. It's a new concept. The barge floats on a lake that it creates as it moves along."

"How on earth does it do that?"

"It digs up the sand in front of it, filters out minerals like zircon, rutile, and silica and drops the filtered sand in back of it. That way it's always floating in its own little pond.

"The problem is, I would only get home for four days

every two weeks. Could you handle that? Of course, I won't know what's required until I go apply for the job. If it's okay with you, I'll go tomorrow."

"Well, if you get the job it will be a long trip back and forth. You would have to take the barge from Dunwich to Cleveland, and then the launch from Redland Bay to here."

"Well…" he paused. "We could send the kids to school on Noyes' boat and I'd use the *Eagle* to go back and forth."

"That's a good idea," I nodded. "The Education Department has already offered to subsidize the kids on Noyes' boat. We could take advantage of that."

Bill got the job and we made arrangements for the children to travel to school on Jack Noyes' boat.

On the first day of this new arrangement, Topper was on deck when the boat approached the Russell Island dock. Without warning, he jumped across to the jetty. At that very moment, the boat lurched. He missed the jetty and dropped into the water. It happened so quickly. Someone sprang to the jetty to hold the launch away from the pilings so he wouldn't get crushed.

Skippy, always quick in an emergency, stretched down and pulled Topper up. Blood was oozing from several places on both legs. He had been cut by the razor sharp oyster shells growing on the pilings.

Mr. Noyes sent the girls home with the message, "Tell your Mom, Skippy and I are taking Topper back to Cleveland for stitches."

"What on earth made Topper do that?" I asked the girls. "He knows better."

"He was trying to copy the big boys," Tia explained. "He's been watching them jump over to the dock to secure the lines when the boat pulls in. He moved so fast I couldn't grab him."

"Mr. Noyes said he'll be right," Pam assured me.

"That's just like Topper, always wanting to help," I told Bill when he rang that night. "In six short years, Topper has had almost as many stitches as a patchwork quilt."

Thankfully, Bill was home when it was time to remove the stitches. We talked about making the long trip to the mainland just to have a doctor snip a few stitches, and then, the long trip home.

"It would be easier if you did the job here," Bill said.

"You've got to be kidding! I'm not a nurse."

"I know you can do it. Let's try. I'll help you."

I took a deep breath, "All right. You put him on the dining room table and I'll get my small scissors and tweezers."

Topper, usually brave, was not happy with the situation. As I began to snip, he started to fuss.

"What is the matter?" I asked.

"I don't want you to take them out," he cried.

"It will only be a minute and it won't hurt," I assured him.

"But my blood will come out," he yelled.

"No, it won't," I tried to calm him. "Now be still. Hon, will you hold him steady for me?" I snipped the stitches on his knee and deftly plucked them out with the tweezers.

"My blood will pump out," he sobbed.

"What *is* the matter, Topper?" It was so unlike him to carry on like this. Bill steadied him while I quickly removed the rest of the stitches on his ankle and calf. "There, you're fine. We've finished. It's all right." I slid him off the table. "Go call the girls and we'll make some popcorn."

When everyone was settled for the night, Bill and I went for a walk. It was therapy time.

"What a day," I said, inhaling the fresh clean air. "I can't imagine what Topper was so upset about."

"I don't understand," Bill said, "he's never complained before."

"Do you suppose it's because I wasn't the doctor?"

"I doubt it," he assured me. We walked on in silence hand-in-hand. I searched my mind, trying to find a connection with blood "pumping out." *Why would that bother him?* I puzzled.

"Oh!" I started to laugh.

"What?" Bill asked.

"Do you remember Topper wanting to know about the heart and what it does? I showed him the human body in the encyclopedia. I told him the heart is like our irrigation pump. I explained that it pumps blood all through our body. He wondered what would happened when the blood was all gone. I assured him that it didn't go away."

"What does that have to do with stitches?" Bill asked.

"Well, when I took the stitches out, he was probably thinking of the irrigation pump running out of water. He was afraid all his blood would pump out through the cuts."

Bill shook his head. "Sounds like Topper all right. He always wants to know how things work."

I sighed with relief. "Tomorrow I'll make sure he understands. Do you think I'm giving him too much information?"

"No," Bill answered, "Topper demands the facts."

*Chapter Eight*

# Looking Ahead

Curtis was right about the sand mining job. The pay was good. The room Bill was given in the employee barracks was more like an efficiency apartment. It had a tiny kitchenette and refrigerator. His first purchase was an electric skillet. Although there was a dining hall, he preferred to cook in his room. When he came home for his first days off, we loaded him up with dishes and cooking supplies. Always having a fondness for cooking, Bill loved creating gourmet meals in his skillet.

"It's the best thing I ever bought," he boasted.

Soon after that, the Routledges moved into a completely furnished company house. After they settled, Daphne rang up to invite us over for a few days.

"Our caravan (Australian for trailer) is empty," she said. "You and the kids can use it while you're here." It was a wonderful. The trailer came with a set of kittens. The girls loved having something to pet, and we all enjoyed their antics.

When he wasn't working, Bill chauffeured us around the island. One day, he drove us up the cliff to Point Lookout.

"This area was named by Captain Cook," he informed us. "In 1770, Cook claimed this area for Great Britain." From Point Lookout, we could see miles out into the Pacific Ocean. We watched the ocean waves roll on to the white sand beaches.

"Perfect spot for surfing," Tia marveled.

Another day, we swam in Brown Lake. Bill, our tour guide, explained, "It's called Brown Lake because the grasses growing there turn the water brown. It's a great place for tourists."

"Does it make the tourists brown?" Topper asked.

"Will it turn us brown?" Pam wanted to know, heading for shore.

"Well, it hasn't turned me brown," Dad laughed. "Come on back in. It's fair dinkum."

The next day, he took us to Blue Lake. It really was blue. A float was anchored about fifty feet off shore. The kids had the time of their lives climbing up and jumping off.

"And no one turned blue," Tia observed at the end of the day.

We visited an Aboriginal burying ground. "There used to be a lot of aborigines on the island," Dad explained. "But as more people came to the island, they gradually drifted away. This burying ground is about all that's left of that era."

## Looking Ahead

Everywhere we went we saw horses roaming free. Even in the streets of Dunwich. "They're wild horses," Bill told us. "They don't belong to anyone, but they don't mind having people around them."

Patting one, Pam observed, "They certainly don't act like they're wild. They came right up to us for a hand-out."

*Petting wild ponies.*

"Do you think these are the same horses that walked around the boys' tents, when they camped over here a few years ago?" Tia asked.

"Could be," Dad said.

"I wish we had horses walking around on Russell Island," Jackie told Daphne at dinner that evening.

"It does seem like fun," Daphne agreed, "but they're a bit of a nuisance because they eat gardens, plants, shrubs, and anything else that isn't fenced in."

"Crikie," Topper exclaimed, "we would need a hundred miles of fence!"

Curtis smiled. "Too right, son."

After dinner and dessert, Daphne showed us pictures of Merran, Kelly, and Ian. They were all grown up. Time passes so quickly. Merran had married and was living across the continent in Perth. "She has two children," Daphne said proudly. "She named her little girl after you, Tia."

As we looked at the pictures, memories came flooding back. I glanced at Curtis.

"Do you remember when you caught a six-foot boa constrictor and gave it to Merran for a pet? She came over to our farm with it in a burlap sack to show it to us. She was so excited about that snake, she could hardly talk."

Curtis laughed. "She had it for almost a year before she decided to turn it loose."

Ah," I sighed, "those were the days. We have such fond memories of our early farming years. Your family was very special to us."

It was a short vacation, but a lot of fun. We enjoyed being with Bill and seeing the island. We had heard so much about it over the years. And, oh yes, when I got home, I made curtains to match Bill's bedspread. Decorating rooms is one of my favorite things to do.

## Looking Ahead

Back at Fiddler's Green, we found a letter waiting for us. Bill's sister had written, urging us to come back to the States. I replied:

*Dear Betty,*

*Thank you for your offer to help us get resettled if we come back to the States. It's very generous of you to consider opening your home to such a crowd of people. You have no idea how everyone has grown.*

*Easter Sunday we went to church on the mainland. I sat in the middle of the family. To the left of me and to the right of me, Moores were spread out as far as I could see. We took up the whole pew! The boys shoulder to shoulder with Bill, and Tia shoulder to shoulder with me. Pam, Jackie, and Topper took up the rest of the pew. Looking at all of them, it was a relief to realize that I have jolly good reasons for my wrinkles and gray hair.*

*In an effort to broaden his eighteen-year-old outlook, Mickey is boarding on the mainland with Ian MacIntyre's family for his senior year. Mickey's a go-getter. He has three after-school jobs: general maintenance at a trailer park, landscape work at the Redland Bay Nursing Home, and walking a neighbor's dog.*

*Skippy has just reached the turmoil of being seventeen. He's doing quite well as the "man in charge" at home. Unfortunately, he is overly stern with the smaller ones in making them toe the line. They are not happy with such heavy-handed authority. This will be an important year for him to decide what he wants to do. He talks about joining the army and serving in an armored division. His other choice is going out West as a "jackeroo." That's an apprentice station manager.*

*Teresa is a delight. I say that quickly because at thirteen one never knows. She started high school this year in the eighth grade. She will begin with general courses and specialize a bit more next year. She needs piano lessons but we haven't been able to find a teacher. Now that we have a piano, we have no teacher.*

*Pam, Jackie, and Topper are all growing, growing, growing. Pam is much quieter and reads a lot. Topper is a bursting ball of energy. He probably won't settle down until he learns to read well enough to satisfy his curiosity. Jackie's bane is her freckles. The three are a trio to be reckoned with. Actually, they are doing extremely well considering their long school days.*

*Bill, as you know, is not happy with Australia. I'm a bit sorry because it's a beautiful country with tremendous potential. I think he would be happier living on the mainland. We have considered the possibility. Since the boys are grown, we need to do something for the girls. I want them to have dancing lessons and be able to join the Girl Scouts. Pam, a champion swimmer, needs the opportunity to compete. These are things that we cannot do on the island.*

*A lot of beautiful homes are being built on the mainland in the Cleveland area. Why don't you move over here? A lovely four-bedroom, brick home* *costs about $20,000. Australian's are big for owning their own homes. Brisbane takes up about the same area as London with a fraction of the people.*

*Australia has its share of strikes and student demonstrations. But it's hard to make a very big splash with only twelve million people in an area about the size of America.*

*Queensland has been scoffed at because of its prudish censorship laws. I'm inclined to say jolly good! It seems that the world badly needs a bit of prudishness. I've heard they censor American novels to such an extent that it's hard to follow the plot. Portnoy's* Complaint *is still banned here. That's not a bad idea when you realize that lowering standards leads… to lower standards.*

*Bill is planning to write to you this week about advertising our place for sale in the US. If we make enough money we'll come back for a visit.*

Within days of sending this letter, there was a knock on the door.

"Who could that be?" I muttered. Grabbing a towel, I wiped my hands as I hurried down the hallway. *No one ever comes to the front door*, I worried, hoping that nothing was wrong. I opened the door to greet a smiling, pleasant-looking chap.

"G'day," he said, "I see you have your property for sale. Is it still available?"

Relieved that it wasn't bad news, I invited him in and made him comfortable in the living room while I prepared the tea tray. Sipping his cup of tea, he explained that he was from

Grantland Consolidated. They would like to make us an offer. I listened to his proposal and said that we would consider it. As he got up to leave, I told him I'd have Bill call him.

That evening when Bill rang, I asked him, "Do you remember a couple of years ago when you said you were waiting for someone to come along and offer us a princely price for this place?"

"I guess so, why?"

"Someone did! Today!" I told him about the offer from Grantland.

"Jolly good!" he said. "Where do I get in touch with this bloke?"

Within a month, papers were drawn up for the sale. We kept two acres with the house, pool, and orchard, just in case we decided to stay on Russell. We also reserved two blocks at the top of the hill overlooking the bay—a great location for a summer cottage. The best part was we could plan on months before any development would begin. We had plenty of time to look at houses on the mainland and to make a decision about moving.

*Chapter Nine*

# Surprise! Surprise!

One day after school, when the other children had eaten their snacks and left, Tia asked, "Mom, what are we going to do for Topper's birthday? He'll be seven years old pretty soon."

"You're right!" I exclaimed. "We had better start making plans. Any ideas?"

"Well, since he goes to school in Cleveland, why don't we invite friends from his class to come over for a party?"

"That's a good idea, but how would they get here? Your dad has the boat at Dunwich."

"They could come on the regular launch."

"I'm not sure their parents would let them do that. Wait a minute... Mickey could go over and be with them on the way back. I'll let their parents know that they will be taken care of on the boat."

I enlisted Mickey to keep Topper occupied while the girls and I had a planning session.

"Pam and I will do the games," Jackie volunteered.

"Jolly good," Pam agreed. "We'll find games in the Pack O' Fun books for boys that age."

"I'll bake a chocolate birthday cake," Tia offered. "That's Topper's favorite. Mom can decorate it with chocolate icing," she finished, smiling at me.

Early the day of the party, we made punch and sandwiches. When it was time to go over to meet the children, Mickey suggested that Topper go with him.

"A great idea," I approved. "Topper is so wound up, I don't know what I'd do with him while you were gone."

As soon as they left, we bustled around putting up decorations and blowing up balloons. Just as we were finishing, there was a faint knock at the door. Opening the door, I looked down at a pint-sized stranger.

"Does Brian Moore live here?" he asked.

"Yes, but he's not here now."

"We came on the boat," another voice piped up from the bottom of the steps.

"Did you come over from Redland Bay?" I asked in amazement.

"Yes," they answered in unison.

"They came on the wrong boat," Jackie said, echoing my thoughts.

I opened the door and ushered in five little boys.

"You've had quite a long walk from the jetty, haven't you? Would you like a drink of lemonade?" Breaking out in smiles, they all nodded. As I poured glasses of lemonade, I wondered, *What next?* Then, I decided to do what I always do in a pinch.

"Pam, go call your father."

I chatted with the boys until Bill poked his head in the door.

"What do you need?" he asked. I explained the situation.

"Oh," he said, "let's go down to the jetty to be there when the other boat comes in."

We loaded everyone on the truck, and drove down to wait for the ferry. I told Bill to park at the top of the hill.

"Want to have some fun?" I asked the boys.

"Yes," five little voices chorused.

"Let's surprise Brian," I said. "We'll hide behind the trees until he comes up the hill. Then we'll jump out and shout 'Happy Birthday!'" They thought that was a great idea and scurried around to find hiding places.

We saw Mickey and Topper get off the boat and plod up the hill. Mickey was wearing a frown and Topper was the essence of dejection. His head was down, his shoulders drooping.

I whispered to Bill, "He must have been heartbroken when no one showed up to come to his party."

Just then, all the boys jumped out from behind the trees shouting, "Happy Birthday, Brian!" Topper's head snapped up. A look of disbelief flooded his face but not for long. He let out a whoop and started running wildly in big circles. It was several minutes before we could calm him down. I have never seen such an excited little boy. It was one birthday he will never forget.

When the party was over and it was time for the boys to go back on the boat, Bill offered to go across with them to apologize to their parents for the boat mix-up.

"They all accepted the apology gracefully," he reported, "but they all said they were confident the boys were in good hands."

Soon after Topper's party, we received a letter from Rusty. He had met a lady whose daughter was in one of his classes and was invited to her home. Mrs. Walters, a mother of three, recognized a lonely soul and took him under her wing. She sent me pictures of her children and Rusty. Excited with the news, I wrote:

> *Dear Mrs. Walters,*
>
> *I can't tell you how much we enjoyed the pictures. We appreciated "meeting" you all. I'll be sending you some family snapshots as soon as I get them developed. It's such a comfort to know that Rusty has wonderful friends. He looks so happy in the pictures.*
>
> *Like most mothers, I tend to worry about him. I don't know if he naturally saves all his complaints for Mom, or if life really is that grim in the U.S. The news reports we get always cover the most dramatic events, riots, demonstrations, and sex. The advertisements for the latest films, American and others, are unbelievably bad. Your letter was encouraging.*
>
> *We're hoping things will go well with Rusty. One hears of so many helicopters being shot down in Vietnam. Right now is not the best time to be a helicopter pilot in the army. But then, no war is a safety zone.*
>
> *Children take such a lot of 'raising,' don't they?*

## Surprise! Surprise!

*Warrant Officer Moore*

Later Rusty wrote that he had passed his helicopter check ride. "I was one of the two highest rated in the flight school," he wrote. He was airborne at last. We were so proud of him. In closing, he mentioned the possibility of his getting leave before going to Vietnam. We were elated with the news, but not sure when to expect him.

"It would be just like Rusty to surprise us," Bill said.

As the Senior Public Exams drew closer, Mickey, living on the mainland, devoted more time to study and his spare time jobs. It became a burden for him to chauffeur the children to and from Redland Bay jetty. Skippy was old enough to get a beginner's permit toward his driving license, but it would be another six months before he could drive without a licensed adult in the car. We solved the problem by arranging for Topper and the girls to travel to Cleveland on the public bus. From the bus station, it was a short walk to the school. Skippy and Tia rode the high school bus. They all met at Redland Bay and came home on Mr. Noyes' boat.

One afternoon, when they boarded the bus, Pam noticed a passenger sitting near the door. "He was wearing 'pointy' boots," she told me later. She glanced up above the boots and saw a white belt with a big buckle. Too shy to look directly at the passenger, she and Jackie scooted to the back of the bus. There they would be free from meddling adults. Keeping an eye on the passenger, they noticed that he kept turning his head to look at them.

Quietly they conferred between themselves. "Do you know who he is?" Pam murmured.

"No, but he looks familiar."

"He looks like he knows us."

"Who do we know around here with red hair?"

"Look! He's getting up. He's coming back here," Jackie whispered.

"Be quiet," Pam shushed.

The stranger sat down on the seat in front of them.

Turning around, he smiled. "Hi! I'm your brother Rusty."

Suddenly a light dawned. "It is, it is!" they shrieked.

Topper piped up, "I knew it! I knew it was Rusty all the time. I was just waiting for him to say something."

Rusty had been given thirty days' leave before being sent to Vietnam. He was attached to a helicopter medi-vac unit. The unit was famous for their swoop in, snatch the wounded, and swoop out operations.

"They call them 'dust-offs,'" Rusty said.

We were so happy to see him again. Two years had seemed like ages. He looked wonderful, a handsome young man. He walked around the farm with his dad. He walked around the island alone, reliving old memories and storing up new ones for the days to come.

The girls showed him all the changes we had made. Mickey and Skippy brought him up to date on his friends and the school. I cooked all of his favorite meals. He went to Redland Bay and spent time with his old school chums—except his fishing pal, Bob Stockwell.

Just five months earlier, Bob had been lost at sea. A fishing boat he was working on went down in a storm. Bob's mother wrote that he often used to say, "I guess the sea will get me one day." The little boy who used to row all the way over to Russell Island by himself, the boy who used to play games with the girls and Canasta with us had lived a short nineteen years. The sea claimed him but he will never be forgotten.

Life is very uncertain. We were painfully aware of that. We had to say goodbye to Rusty once more. But not for the last time, we vowed. He assured us that everything would be fine. We trusted God that he was right.

*Chapter Ten*

# Mickey Grows Up

In Australia, a Senior Pass is the equivalent of a high school diploma. Final exams are a lengthy process of six term papers over a period of three weeks. Australians use the term "sit for exams" because that's what the students do. They sit for hours writing page after page. No multiple choice questions here. No graduation events either. Students simply proceed to the next stage of their lives.

Mickey sat for his Senior Public Exam in November. The results wouldn't be announced until January, but he was confident he had made the grade. Looking for something to do in the meantime, he proposed a project.

"We've done everything to improve Fiddler's Green except for one thing," he told me.

"Fair dinkum, what's that?"

"The shed. Remember how Dad always wanted to build a new one? Well, he can't now because he's working on Stradbroke." Then he added, with his I-know-you-can't-turn-me-down look, "I want to give it a go if it's all right with you."

"Michael James," I laughed, "you presented your case very well. You've been building one thing or another all your life. Go ahead and try it. Even though we've sold the farm, we don't know how long we'll be here. Dad's four days off start tomorrow. Talk it over with him."

Bill approved of the project. They began to make plans. "We have trees up in the woods just the right size for posts. Gerard will help you cut them down and strip the bark. Get those ready first," he suggested, "then do a coat of termite protection. While that's drying, you can clean out the shed."

The old shed held at least fifty year's accumulation of parts and pieces. Sorting through all the junk was an exciting challenge for Mickey. Digging postholes was another thing. Hearing groans and moans from the shed, I went out to see what was going on. Mickey was chipping away at the hard-packed dirt floor with a pickax.

"It would be less work trying to make a hole in cement," he grunted.

Stopping to wipe his brow, he told me he would be putting up the rafters as soon as the posts were set.

"They'll be easier," he said. "I'm going to use a hand drill with a circular saw attachment to cut the timber. Once I get the roof framed, Skippy and Gerard said they would help me. We'll nail corrugated tin onto the top and sides of the building."

Enthusiastically, he described his plans for the inside. "The floor will be a split-level configuration made from ant bed. Crushed and rolled, ant bed makes a great floor. One side of the shed will be for the tractor. The other side will be for storage and a much-needed workshop. For a final touch, I plan to build lots of shelves and work benches."

It was all Greek to me, but I admired his planning and his determination. "Sounds great," I said. "How about some milk and cookies? You'll be needing lots of energy for all that work."

Skippy helped with the project when he wasn't busy with farm chores. Gerard often came by to lend a hand. But with or without help, Mickey worked on undaunted. Finishing his first real building was a great accomplishment for him.

Showing us the results, he grinned with pride. "This replacement isn't any ordinary shed," he reckoned. "It's twenty-five by forty feet and better than anything I could ever have imagined."

Delighted, we congratulated him on a job well done. His dad, patting him on the shoulder, declared, "It's a great improvement for Fiddler's Green. You've done well."

I did what mothers do… I made his favorite dessert for dinner.

With that massive project under his belt, Mickey was invited to visit the Barfields in Mackay.

"I think I'll look for a job while I'm up there," he mentioned before he left. "I'd like to work a year before going to teacher's college."

With Uncle Tom's encouragement, he applied for a job at the Mackay Main Roads Department. Back from his vacation, he told us he was hoping for an opening with a

Surveying Crew. In preparation, he bought a 1954 Prefect from Topper's teacher.

A week later, he had good news. Returning with the mail, he ran up the stairs waving a letter in the air. "I got the job!" he shouted.

When he was seventeen, I couldn't wait for Mickey to grow up. But now my life was changing dramatically. How does a mother feel when her children become adults? It's hard to explain. On the outside, I was happy for him. On the inside, I ached. First Rusty, then Mickey. My little boys were no longer "my little boys." Time goes forward, not backward. Mom would have to adapt.

"Wonderful," I said striving to sound enthusiastic. "When do you leave?"

"Next week. Uncle Tom told me I could stay with him until I find a place. Too bad I can't take my car." He had discovered that the little British car, with a stick shift, didn't have enough power to climb steep hills.

"What are you going to do for transportation?" I asked.

"Don't know," he said, "but I'll think of something. In the meantime, I'll travel by bus."

I smiled, remembering what it was like to be young. When you're young, nothing is impossible.

Within a few days, he was packed and ready to go.

"I'll be taking a bus at Redland Bay," he explained. "There is no reason for you to make the trip over." We settled for waving goodbye at the jetty. With a heavy heart, I watched one more son step into manhood.

Happily, good news arrived with his first letter. He hadn't been on the job long before they put him in charge of planning, buying, and cooking meals for the crew.

"As camp cook, I have my own trailer," he wrote, "it's a beaut." He loved the opportunity to indulge in one of his favorite pastimes—comparison shopping. Challenging himself to provide the crew with the best meals at the lowest price, he earned a "she's right, mate" (Australian for "good job") from a satisfied, well-fed gang.

Following his big brother's example, he saved money to buy a motorcycle, just as Rusty had done at that age. It wasn't long before he traded his motorcycle for a much better car. "You can have the Prefect," he wrote to his dad.

Bill took the Prefect over to Dunwich on the barge. In his spare time, he dismantled it and put it back together.

"That four-cylinder engine was so small I lifted it out of the car by myself," he told me. "No wonder it wouldn't go up steep hills." He drove the car around Stradbroke for a while and then sent it back to Russell Island. "I don't really need a car over here," he said.

It did come in handy for us. Gerard used it to drive the children to and from the school boat. At least, I thought that was all he was doing. Until one afternoon, Topper came home bursting with excitement.

"Guess what, Mom?" he called, running up the stairs.

"What?" I asked, putting out cookies and milk.

"I drove the car home!"

"You what?" My gaze swung to Gerard, who had followed him up the stairs.

Lowering his eyes apologetically, Gerard spoke softly. "I was going to tell you I've been teaching him to drive." He looked up at me. "You never know when it will come in handy. Topper is only seven, but he has a good head on his shoulders."

Gerard had spent enough time in the Outback to know that children need to be prepared for emergencies. He had already taught Pam and Jackie to drive. It didn't bother me too much, because he was always right there with them. Except the day Gerard was away. Skippy, taking advantage of their driving skills, sent the two girls down to get their dad who was coming home by boat.

Bill had moored the *Eagle* and was walking along the jetty when he saw the Prefect coming down the hill. Knowing Gerard was away, he supposed Skippy was behind the wheel. When he drew closer, he got the shock of his life. All he could see was Jackie's blue eyes peeking over a steering wheel held by two tiny hands. He could barely see Pam, sitting smugly beside her.

"Where's Skippy?" he asked reaching for the door.

"Skippy was busy. He told us to come get you," Pam explained, scooting over to give him room.

He looked at Jackie. "Just because you're ten years old doesn't mean you can drive a car all by yourself," he scolded.

"Skippy said so," she defended herself.

"I'll have a talk with Skippy when I get home," Bill frowned, " but I don't want either of you to drive this car again unless Gerard is with you."

"Yes, sir," they answered respectfully. But with Dad at the wheel, they turned their heads and grinned at each other, relishing their accomplishment.

*Chapter Eleven*

# Summer Travel, Summer TV

With the two boys and Bill away most of the time, Gerard became our handyman.

One day, he suggested, "Now that the shed is done, why don't you take a camping trip out my way? I'll be going home to Warwick in a couple of weeks."

"Can we, Mom?" Topper asked, sensing a new adventure.

"It would be a jolly good thing to do, wouldn't it? And it's only a few hours away. I'll talk to your dad when he comes home."

"Maybe we can ride the horses," Jackie beamed. She knew that Gerard had connections with a lot of cattle stations in Warwick. She reckoned that where there were cattle, horses couldn't be far away.

"I want to go too," Pam joined the conversation from her bedroom. She didn't care where we were going—just don't leave her at home.

Tia poked her head around the door. "Where are we going, Gerard?"

"Down to the jetty to get your dad," I answered for him. "Gerard, it's almost time for the boat. Would you mind taking the kids along? Tia can help me get dinner while I answer her question."

While Tia set the table, I told her about Gerard suggesting a camping trip to his hometown. "We'll have to ask Dad first."

"Dad's home now," she said. Before she could reach the door, the three young ones burst in, yelling, "We can go! We can go!"

By the time we finished the last bit of peanut butter ice cream, the trip had been planned. Toowoomba, the garden city—our first stop. Gerard—our guide. Bill, who had four days off from work, made plans to connect with us at Cleveland on the weekend. During the week, we busied ourselves organizing the food and camping gear. By Friday, we were packed and ready to go.

At Redland Bay, we loaded our supplies into the station wagon and drove to Cleveland just before Bill arrived on the Dunwich barge. Gerard moved to the back seat with the kids, and Bill settled himself in the driver's seat. We were off on another adventure.

"What a pleasant change," I sighed, watching the scenery pass by. "Here we are, rolling along a road that is more than seven miles long. Imagine, all the people in those houses can go to school or shop—without having to take a boat. What an interesting concept."

We pulled into the camping area just as the sun was finishing its day. With one quick swoop, Gerard spread out his drover's sleeping roll. Ready for the night, he collected kindling, started a fire, and put the billy on to boil.

I nudged Bill and nodded in Gerard's direction, "I think we're going to learn a lot about camping on this trip."

Still sorting out tent poles, pegs, and tie downs, Bill observed, "Gerard doesn't travel with a wife and family."

Early to bed, and even earlier to rise, we ate a hasty breakfast and broke camp. Gerard guided us on a tour of Toowoomba, a modern pastoral town on the Darling Downs. As we neared Picnic Point, with its mushroom-shaped water tower, Gerard asked Bill to pull up to a little shop.

"I'll be right back," he drawled, climbing out of the car. Minutes later, he reappeared with a huge watermelon. "Park over there by that shade tree," he pointed. "We'll cool our thirst," he said with a grin.

Later that day, when we were hot and dusty, Gerard called a stop for another watermelon. Again, we sat in the shade of a big tree enjoying the cool sweet slices. They brightened our eyes and renewed our energy.

Bill leaned over to me and murmured, "We are learning a few things from Gerard, aren't we?" I smiled.

That evening, we camped by Sandy Creek. The creek was dotted with ten-foot high granite boulders. Over many years, the rushing river had washed them round and smooth as pebbles. At that time, the creek was shallow enough for the children to wade in. We sat on the bank until dusk, watching them play in the water and climb the boulders.

"On our way back" Gerard ventured, "we'll pass through Cunningham's Gap."

"I know about Cunningham's Gap," Tia said. "We studied it in school. It was discovered by explorers traveling

*Watermelon Safari*

west, many years ago. The Gap," she continued, "opened the way across the mountains, to the grassy western plains, where they could raise cattle and crops. It's like America's Cumberland Gap through the Appalachians, that opened the West in America." she finished.

"Righto," Gerard agreed. "That's what the Darling Downs is all about—cattle and crops. It seems that America and Australia have a lot in common."

At Warwick we spent an afternoon with Gerard's family. Although he had never married, he was very proud of his numerous nieces and nephews. Several of them, the ages of our children, showed the kids around the farm. The horses were the greatest attraction. Gerard gave each of the children a ride and then lined them all up on one horse for a picture.

The whole trip was interspersed with unforgettable watermelon stops. It was a wonderful vacation. We had explored another corner of this great continent. We dubbed our trip the "Watermelon Safari."

Back at Fiddler's Green, we found a welcomed letter from Mickey. "I've joined the church youth group," he wrote. "I play ping pong and work with sub-normal children." His next sentence was a jolt. "I made a 'layby' on a television set. After I wrote that, I covered my ears. I knew Mom would yell loud enough to be heard all the way to Mackay." Of course I didn't yell, but he certainly understood how I felt about televisions.

I was thankful to have been able to raise the children through their formative years without television invading their lives and twisting their values. They were so busy doing other things, it didn't bother them—until they went to school on the mainland. Then the girls began to complain.

"We don't know what our friends in school are talking about because we don't have a television," Jackie protested.

"That's right," Tia said. "It's hard."

During our walk-talk time that evening, I told Bill about the problem.

"I know it's difficult," he sympathized, "but what can we do?"

"Would it possible to rent a television set for one week?" I mused, with my thought machine cranked up full speed.

"You would do that?" he asked in amazement. He was well aware of my feelings about television.

"For a week? Yes. We'll let them choose what they want to watch—within reason, of course. Then it goes back."

When vacation started, Bill went to the mainland and brought home a television set. What excitement! Bill and I watched the news while the children ate. They watched all the shows their friends had talked about. During commercials, they ran to do their chores. The hallway between the kitchen and living room got a wonderful shine as they skated back and forth in their socks.

After the first day back at school, they arrived home full of satisfaction. "I knew what Marie was talking about today," Jackie said happily. "I told her I really loved that show."

"Me too," laughed Pam. "We talked about the Lucy show."

"It was good, Mom," Tia said dropping her port and giving me a hug. "Thanks for renting the television set. It helped a lot."

We did the same thing the following summer. After the television went back, Bill said, "You know... I reckon it would be cheaper if we rented it for a month."

"Fair dinkum?"

"Yes, and it wouldn't be as hectic."

"Well, they have done well in choosing shows. I suppose we could try that next year. That will be the big test."

The following summer we had television for a whole month. We scheduled watching to cover just about everything it offered. Most of the shows were from America. The whole family enjoyed it thoroughly.

Strangely though, we all heaved a collective sigh of relief when it was gone. It had been fun while it lasted, but we were happy to have our lives back under *our* control.

*Chapter Twelve*

# The Gift of Time

When I went back to Brisbane for my doctor's appointment, he said, "You will need an operation. There may be more than I can see under the circumstances. But we won't know until we operate."

Twenty years ago, my mother heard a similar message from her doctor. The unspoken word was "cancer." Despite weeks of painful treatment, she died less than a year later. Many times as I grew up, I heard these words, "You're so much like your mother."

*Was I to follow my mother to an early grave?* I wondered.

Death is something I thought about often. My body had never been robust. Sickness robbed me of much of my childhood. A bad fall when I was nine left me with a constant pain in my hip. "When she grows up, she'll need a lift on her shoe," the doctor told my mother when I complained about the pain. "And when she gets older," he added, "perhaps a wheelchair."

Did he think a ten-year-old had no ears and couldn't hear? I never mentioned the pain again. No doctor was going to put a lift on my shoe! I wrestled with the pain alone. Each birthday I celebrated a victory over circumstances. I could still walk tall!

When I became a mother, my daily prayer was, "Lord, let me live until my children are old enough to take care of themselves. I don't want to have someone else bring them up. They're mine. You gave them to me."

I focused on making them independent. I called it "chores," but it was a march toward self-sufficiency. It started when our first little boy was eighteen-months-old. Bill put a clothes hook twenty inches above the floor right beside Rusty's closet. "This is where you hang up your pajamas," he explained. We cheered him on as he learned to make it a daily achievement.

When he was two-years-old, Bill made a set of low shelves. "This is where you put your toys away." We played the pick up game with him until he was able to do it by himself. At three, he learned his first chore. "Now you're a big boy, you can help mommy empty the waste baskets."

At four, I used his bedspread in place of the top sheet. "This is how you make your bed." It wasn't difficult to smooth the spread and was worth all the praise he received for a good job. The march toward self-sufficiency went on with all the children—cookie baking, meals, cleaning up, laundry, ironing, and sewing.

My strategy was to build independence step by step. Always with the prayer, "Please, God, one more year.

They're almost ready to manage without me." Each birthday was another celebration of time granted. I passed the dreaded fortieth with relief. *Perhaps this time*, I thought, *I'll not be like my mother. Perhaps I can hope for a future.*

These thoughts played across my mind as I sat on the home-bound ferry boat. I was 41. *How can I tell Bill?* I wondered. It's not the shoe-lift. It's not the wheelchair. It's not the pain. They're old friends. We have been acquainted for years and have learned to live together. This is different.

For twenty years, I had kept this specter locked up with the hurt of my mother's death. When it tried to invade my life by telling me, "You take after your mother," I slammed the door, shutting it out. But now, I had to face it squarely. *Thank you, Lord, for the years I've had. Thank you that my children are old enough to manage without me—if that is what must be.*

When he called that night, Bill's first question was, "What did the doctor say?"

"He said I need an operation. I wouldn't be able to have children anymore."

"Is it really that bad?" he asked in a low voice. To comfort me, he added, "Well, we already decided that Topper was an extra dividend."

"I know. I guess it has to be done. But I don't want to do anything until the children are back in school."

"Will it be all right to wait?"

"Yes, the doctor scheduled me right after school starts. He said it's best not to put it off any longer."

I was able to explain the situation to the children without alarming them. Fortunately, they were more focused on preparing for the new school year. I had a few days to hear about their teachers and classes before I left for the hospital. Seeing them happy and excited about the future, I was able to relax.

Lying on the gurney waiting for the operating room to be ready, I prayed silently. The anesthesiologist sitting beside me stood up, leaned close, and asked, "Are you all right?"

"Yes," I nodded smiling. He could not understand why I was so calm. But I had peace beyond understanding. I read in the Bible that this kind of peace was a gift from God.

A few minutes later, he stood up again and asked, "Are you sure you're all right?" I nodded. "It's time to go," he said, pushing the gurney forward. "They're ready for us." The operating team took over and I faded into a deep sleep.

Hours later, reentering the real world, I waited for the doctor's verdict. When he made his afternoon rounds, he assured me, "The operation went well. We're having tissue tested and we'll let you know as soon as the results come back."

A week later Bill came from Stradbroke to take me home. "The doctor says it will take six months to fully recover," I told him. "He said if I try to rush it, there may be problems later."

"Promise me you'll stay in bed and rest," he demanded, leading me into the bedroom.

"After the long ride from Brisbane, sitting on a bench on the ferry, and the bumpy drive from the jetty, that's an easy promise to make," I groaned.

"I'm sorry about all that," he said, tucking me in, "but I'm so glad you're home."

"So am I." I smiled at him to let him know it was okay.

"Tia, Pam, Jackie, and Topper will take care of you and the house," he said, as he was getting ready to go back to Stradbroke. "Skippy is in charge of everything else."

Two days later, the wind began to gust. Bill rang, "Could you have Skip go down to jetty to check on the *Seagull*? I reckon we're going to crop a bit of weather. They say a typhoon is approaching."

Skippy, looking for adventure, was off down the road in a flash. Even though we never used the *Seagull*, it was still anchored offshore.

Lying in bed, I kept hearing a squeaking noise. It was like fingernails on chalkboard. I struggled out of bed to investigate. The sound was coming from the corner of the roof. As I watched through the window, the wind lifted a panel and dropped it down again. The screeching was metal rubbing on metal as it pulled against the nails that held it. I tried not to think of Padden's roof that had blown off a few years before.

The wind was getting stronger, "Where could Skippy be? He's been gone too long," I moaned. Shuffling slowly to the bathroom window, I looked out on the driveway. No Skippy in sight. *I'll give him another ten minutes*, I reasoned. *Then I'll send the girls to check on him before the storm gets worse.* By now, I was steadily pacing from one window to another.

I could wait no longer. "Tia, would you and Pam walk down to the jetty to look for Skippy? If you don't see him, come right back and let me know. Jackie and Topper will stay here with me." I laid down for a few minutes, trying to stay calm. I couldn't. I got up and began to pace from window to window, feeling totally helpless.

*What could have happened?* I fretted to myself, staring out at the driveway. My heart skipped a beat. Tia and Pam were coming around the corner of the shed. But where was Skippy? Was he all right? What kind of news were they bringing?

Movement, at the far end of the shed, caught my eye. Skippy was creeping along, staying out of sight of the girls. I opened the door as they came up the steps.

"We couldn't find Skippy and there's going to be a typhoon," Tia said with a worried frown.

"It's all right," I soothed, giving her a hug. "He's right behind you."

Skippy thought it was all a game. He told us he had been sheltering at the school when they went by and decided to play a trick on them. He thought it was funny.

"It wasn't funny," Pam shouted at him. "The wind almost blew me away!"

"That was mean," Tia said, "making us walk all the way to the jetty. We almost couldn't get back up the hill. You worried Mom, too." They turned their backs on Skippy and walked away. That was all the scolding he needed.

Chagrined, he said quietly, "The boat's okay, Mom." Skippy means well, but he doesn't always count the cost.

"Thank you, Skip," I murmured, shuffling wearily back to bed.

As I listened to the roof protesting the wind, I thanked God that everyone was home safe and prayed that the roof would not be blown off. *This is certainly not the worst day of my life,* I thought, *but it ranks close.* Although the wind shrieked and moaned most of the night, our house remained intact. We were blessed.

On my next visit to the hospital, the doctor announced, "No sign of cancer." One more answered prayer. God is good indeed.

*Chapter Thirteen*

# A New Journey

By the end of summer, the land sale was finalized. Sitting in the gazebo one Sunday, we talked about what to do next. We had decided to keep the house with an acre of land and two blocks at the top of the hill.

"A perfect spot for a retirement home," I said. "True, it will be years before we get to that stage, but there's no harm in planning ahead."

"Speaking of planning ahead," Bill said, "do you realize we've been in Australia close to ten years?"

"Ten years!" I yelped, almost spilling my coffee. My thoughts raced back through time. How had the years passed by so quickly? I stared into space as my mind swept through ten years of memories.

"Remember the promise we made when we left the States?" Bill asked, bringing me back to the present.

"Yes, I do. I was just thinking about that. We told everyone we would come back for a visit after ten years." I paused, reminiscing. Finally, I spoke, "Our families have never seen Jackie or Pam, they were born in Japan. Even though we lived in California a year before we left for Australia, no one in the family was able to visit us. The children need to know our homeland. Especially our little Australian boy."

"Too right," Bill said, draining his coffee, "I guess it's time to make that visit. Let's talk to the boys," he suggested. "You ring up Mickey and I'll go find Skippy."

Mickey told us he had done a lot of traveling and wanted to stay on at his job in Mackay. Skippy was in the middle of his last year at school.

"I need to finish Senior," he said. "I can travel later." That made sense. Besides, he would be able keep an eye on the farm and be company for Aunt Jac.

With that settled, I volunteered to be in charge of wardrobes. "Since that's my job anyway," I told Bill.

"Jolly good," he quipped. "I just can't see myself designing and sewing clothes, so I'll volunteer to be in charge of travel."

I laughed, "Rather you than me." We began to plan.

After searching through a pile of maps and making notes, Bill came to me with a report. "We'll take a ship to Florida…"

I interrupted with a question, "You mean straight to Florida?"

He rolled his eyes and sighed. He had forgotten geography wasn't my best subject.

Patiently, he began again, "We'll take a ship that stops at New Zealand, Fiji, and Mexico. From there, we'll go south to pass through the Panama Canal and on to Florida. When we arrive there, we will rent a car and stop at Disney World on the way to my sister's house in South Carolina. I'll write and ask Marlin if he would try to locate a used van that we can purchase for the rest of our trip."

"That makes good sense," I smiled. "The kids will love all those places, especially Disney World. What else have you planned so I can decide what we'll need for clothes?"

He unfolded a map of the U.S. "I want the children to see as much of America as possible, so I'm planning a camping tour." Tracing the route with his finger, he explained that we would be traveling through thirty-three states and parts of Canada.

"Camping sounds like fun," I agreed. "We can be very independent and flexible that way. You're doing a great job."

The girls and I rummaged through the latest pattern books. They chose their favorite styles and colors. We planned a shopping trip to buy yardage, and I began to sew. In a few weeks, we had a wardrobe of dresses, slack suits, shorts, blouses, bathrobes, and purses. We bought Bill's shirts and our shoes.

"It cost $200.00 to outfit us all," I told Bill proudly. "See what you can accomplish," I encouraged the girls, "if you learn to make things yourself."

Bill booked us on the Greek ship, *S.S. Australis*, scheduled to sail from Sydney to Port Everglades, Florida. Since it was wintertime and the middle of the school year, I registered the children in Correspondence School. The school arranged for study materials to follow us on the trip. Completed lessons would be sent back for corrections and comments.

We packed the necessary camping equipment and set sail on July 30, 1972. Once on the ship, it didn't take us long to notice that the *S.S. Australis* was not a luxury liner. It was clean, the food was plentiful, but no extras and little emphasis on entertainment. We worked out a schedule for the three-week trip. The children spent the mornings doing their lessons and afternoons in the pool.

"This is beaut," Pam said, floating in the water. "Back in Australia, it's still winter."

At New Zealand, our first port, we revisited their famous zoo. This time a baby hippo was the star. New Zealand has few native animals but many native birds, especially their national emblem, the kiwi. Nocturnal and very shy, kiwis are seldom seen during the day. On our way over to Australia, one of the zoo keepers brought out a kiwi to show us. It was daytime, so the kiwi wasn't feeling too peppy. Even so, it was a great treat to see a real live New Zealand kiwi.

After the zoo, Bill suggested we take a bus.

"I want to see the Auckland War Memorial Museum again," he explained. He was fascinated with a huge dugout canoe. It was a replica of the canoes the Maoris used hundreds of years ago in traveling from Polynesia to New Zealand.

"Imagine," he marveled, "sailing over a thousand miles on the open ocean in one of these."

"Fair dinkum, Daddy!" Topper piped up. "We'd better not complain about the *S.S. Australis*."

"Mom, look at this," Tia called. It was a statue of a Gilbert Island warrior. "His armor is made of woven reed mats," she noted, reading the sign. "And look at his helmet—it's made from a porcupine-fish."

"Truly amazing," I agreed. "Things certainly were different long ago, weren't they?"

From there, we toured Auckland by bus and stopped at the city hall to attend a Maori Concert. It was very impressive. All the singers were dressed in bright floral sarongs. They kept time by stomping their right foot, while clapping or waving their hands above their heads. Although we didn't understand the words, we enjoyed their lovely melodic voices.

Twelve days later, we docked at Acapulco, Mexico. Acapulco's greatest asset was a deep harbor that allows safe anchor for big ships. Although the shoreline was dotted with rich homes and beautiful hotels, further inland things were different. We saw maize crops planted up steep hills without the benefit of terracing. Houses were simple, sometimes only reed huts, with pigs roaming in the yards. Mexicans are a poor race with great artistic skills. It was common to see them selling beautiful handicrafts on the sidewalks.

"It's a good thing we don't have any room in our luggage," I told Bill, "or I would be buying all of next year's Christmas gifts right here."

He took my arm and steered me into the nearest Mexican restaurant.

"The kids are hungry," he said, to refocus my thinking.

After a delicious lunch, we went to the El Mirador Hotel to watch the death-defying high divers. Their dives, from the top of a cliff, must be timed with the exact movement of the waves rushing into the cove below.

"Not a job I would want," I told Bill.

It was almost dark by the time we returned to the beach to wait for a small boat to ferry us back to the ship.

Even though a gentle rain was falling, Topper shouted, "Let's go for a swim! We've got our bathing togs."

Alas! There were no changing rooms available. Being Moores, the kids improvised. With wrap-around towels, they managed to don their togs and dash for the water. Tia and I sheltered under one of the reed umbrellas that dotted the beach.

I noticed a young man under a nearby umbrella, who was obviously enjoying the antics of the children. Catching my eye, he nodded. Knowing that Bill was close by, I smiled politely. That started one of the high spots of my visit to Acapulco.

Taking my smile as an invitation, the young man joined us under our umbrella. He was Greek and spoke only a few words of English. We sat on the sand drawing pictures and using hand motions to communicate. He pointed to himself and wrote "Viro" in the sand. I pointed to myself and wrote "Connie."

I learned that he was the first cook aboard our ship. He loved children. He explained that he was not married by pointing to my wedding ring, then to himself and shaking his head. He conveyed that Greek men do not look for a wife until they're older. He wrote 27 in the sand. I nodded my head in understanding.

He told me that jobs were hard to get in his country. He was lucky to be on the ship. Until the swimmers decided to call it a day, we talked on, comparing life in Greece and America.

Wet, sandy, and shoeless, we headed back to the *Australis* in one of the ship's lifeboats. That evening, we waved to Viro as we passed through the buffet line. He grinned and nudged the chef beside him. We were special friends, his look said.

## A New Journey

Five days later, on deck before dawn, we watched Panama City rise out of the mist. Navigating through the canal was the most exciting part of the whole trip. I paced back and forth from bow to stern, taking in every magnificent detail. Bill and I watched locomotives pull the ship into one of the locks.

"It will take eight hours to cross to the Atlantic Ocean," Bill explained, as the huge steel doors closed us into the lock and the water began to rise.

"Imagine," I said in awe, "a huge ship climbing steps of water to reach a lake, and then descending steps of water into another ocean!"

"Before the canal was built," my information expert continued, "ships had to go around the tip of South America. The trip from San Francisco to New York was 13,000 miles. With the canal, it's only 5,000 miles."

"You are so smart," I praised. "Now, I have some interesting information for you."

"What's that?" he wondered.

I grinned. "Thanks to this wonderful canal, in three more days, we'll be in America!"

*Chapter Fourteen*

# Hello America!

"Hurry, let's go up on deck," Bill urged as we finished breakfast. "We'll be seeing land soon."

"Gosh," Tia said, "I can't wait to see cousin Jani. She's just my age. But I don't remember much about America at all."

"I've never ever seen it," Topper complained, leaning on the rail, searching the horizon.

"There it is!" Jackie shouted, pointing to a distant skyscraper.

"Righto!" Pam exclaimed.

We stayed on deck enjoying the scenery as the boat inched into its Fort Lauderdale berth. After it tied up, we were told that it would take another three hours before permission would be given to go ashore. An old shipmate of Bill's had arranged to meet us when we arrived. Scanning the crowd on the dock, Bill spotted Kilby Taylor and his wife, Vivian. All we could do was wave at each other. Slowly, the hours passed.

Finally, we were processed through customs. When we got together, Kilby explained the delay.

"There's a big GOP convention in Fort Lauderdale," he told us. "It means a lot more security checks than usual."

"That's why it took so long," Vivian explained. "We're so glad you finally got off the ship. I'm sure the children were anxious to actually land in America. You have a lovely family."

While we answered questions about living in Australia, Bill excused himself to arrange for a rental car. He returned in a few minutes with a worried look.

"What's the matter?" I asked.

"There are no cars available to rent because of the convention."

"Oh, no!" Pam wailed. "How will we get to Disney World?"

"Don't worry," Bill soothed her. "I know we planned to go there on the way to South Carolina, but now we'll have to work out something else."

We held a quick conference and decided to go to South Carolina by train. We loaded as much luggage as we could into the Taylor's car. The children were happy to stay on the dock with the rest of our suitcases while we went to the train station.

Locating the station was not an easy task. There were no directional signs, and the Taylors weren't familiar with the area. Bill hailed a passing truck driver for help. Maybe it was his heavy Southern drawl that confused us. We found ourselves going around in circles.

"I guess people don't travel by train anymore," I told Vivian. "I haven't seen one sign indicating a railroad station."

Finally, the pickup truck we had passed twice beeped at us.

"Did y'all find the station?" the driver called out the window. We shook our heads.

"Follow me," he said. Within minutes, he pointed to a tiny, dingy building. Making sure we understood that it was the train station, he drove off as we waved our thanks.

"What a blessing," I breathed in relief. "He may not have looked like an angel, but I'm sure he was one."

Bill inquired about tickets to Columbia, South Carolina while we unloaded the luggage.

"The train is full and it pulls out in twenty-five minutes," a stocky porter told him. "Next train is tomorrow afternoon."

"We just came from Port Everglades and need six seats for two adults and four children," Bill pleaded.

Perhaps it was his Aussie accent that saved the day. The porter checked with the station master and came up with six tickets.

"These are the last seats available and we leave in 20 minutes," he said.

Vivian and I stayed with the luggage while Bill and Kilby raced back to the ship. I kept glancing at my watch. The people on the platform, waiting to board, thinned out until we were the only ones left.

"Dear Lord," I prayed, "don't let Bill and Kilby get lost again." The conductor on the train steps kept looking at us, then at his watch.

"Don't worry," Vivian whispered, "it'll be all right."

"How many miles is it to Port Everglades?" I asked.

"I'm not sure," she said, "but it's not too far."

We had three minutes left, part of our luggage was aboard, and the train was getting ready to leave.

"If I was a fingernail chewer," I told Vivian, "mine would all be nubs by now."

"Look!" she shouted, pointing over my shoulder. "There they are!"

"Jolly good!" I cried with relief.

Rushing the rest of the luggage aboard, we thanked the Taylors for their help and patience.

"Without you two we would have been sitting in the station all night. You've been wonderful," I said, as we hugged goodbye.

It had taken two carloads to transport the six of us and twenty pieces of luggage. Kilby called to Bill as we climbed aboard, "I'll phone your sister and tell her she'll need more than one car to pick up you and your mountain of luggage."

"Too right," we laughed, waving goodbye. The whistle blew and the train chugged out of the station. As soon as we settled into our seats, we realized we hadn't eaten for hours. Everyone was starving. Fortunately, the conductor announced, "The dining car is open." The Moores were the first in line.

In Columbia, Marlin and Betty met us with their car and "our" van. After hugs all around, Marlin related the story of his search for the van.

"They're so hard to find right now," he said. "I even put my business card on van windshields in parking lots. Last week, in desperation, I saw a man getting into this one outside of the Post Exchange. I went over and told him about my problem." Marlin finished with a satisfied grin, "I talked him into selling it."

Bill and I walked around the Volkswagen Kombi Van. It wasn't quite like the one we had crossed Australia in, but it did have a split front seat. There was no zip-on awning but it was roomy enough for all of our luggage, camping equipment, and children.

"It's going to be perfect," I announced.

Driving through Columbia, we saw a city of lovely tree-shaded suburbs. The brick houses seemed to belong to the landscape. Betty told us air conditioning had become standard equipment. We noticed in particular the good manners of people we met. "Please," "thank you," and "excuse me" were heard often.

Cousin Jani and Bill's mother rushed out of the house to welcome us when we arrived. How is it, when we get older, it surprises us that other people do too? We had become accustomed to our own gray hairs. We were not prepared to see his mother's crown of white. Jani, the cute little five-year-old, was now a beautiful young teen with dark auburn hair.

As we rushed to greet them, I nudged Bill, "Ten years does make a difference, doesn't it?"

A few days later, after things had settled down, Betty put her arm around her brother.

"I have a favor to ask," she said. "Marlin won a cruise at work. It's on a ship going to the Bahamas. Would you mind staying with mother and Jani for a couple of days while we're away?"

"Of course not," Bill said. "We promised to take the kids to Disney World tomorrow, but we'll be back in plenty of time."

The Magic Kingdom was just that. It had been open only a year. The workers were young and enthusiastic. There was endless entertainment on the streets during the short waits between rides. The children were enthralled. It was almost more than they could take in. Happily wrapped up in the kingdom's magic, we started back to South Carolina to keep our promise to Betty.

Driving on the super highway through Georgia, the van hiccuped and stopped running. Bill coasted to the side of the road.

"What's wrong?" I asked.

"Something's crook," he said. "I'll go take a look." We all piled out of the van, waiting for the verdict.

Bill shook his head, "It's the motor. I think it blew a connecting rod."

"Fair dinkum, is that bad?" I asked. "We're supposed to be back in South Carolina this afternoon."

He frowned and shrugged his shoulders. "It means we aren't going anywhere until we can get towed to a garage."

While we were wondering what to do next, a big semi trailer pulled off the highway and came to a stop behind us.

"Y'all need some help?" the driver called, climbing down from his cab. Bill told him about our problem, explaining our need to get back to South Carolina.

The driver took off his hat and scratched his head in thought. Putting it back on, he drawled, "I could give the Missus and the young'uns a ride to the train station in Savannah. They'd be able to git to Columbia from thar. If y'all wait here, I'll notify a garage to come out with a tow."

I looked at Bill. He was waiting for me to make the decision. I looked up at that big truck. I looked at the driver. I wasn't keen about riding off with a perfect stranger, but there seemed to be no other option.

"Thank you," I said, glancing at Bill who nodded his approval. "I appreciate your offer very much."

Smiling, the driver lifted the children into the semi. "You young'uns can fit on the bench-seat in back, yer maw can sit here in front."

I took a deep breath. *Here we go on another great adventure*, I thought, climbing up into the truck cab. The children were thrilled to be riding in a big semi rig. They could see so much more of the road and countryside. They chatted happily from their perch.

To calm my apprehension, I talked with the driver about his work.

"I like ta git ta places," he drawled. "But they's times when I hafta make a real long haul. That's why I gut those." He pointed to a little white box on the tray between the seats. Them's m' pills," he grinned. "I ain't 'posed to have 'em, they says, but I shur do need 'em at times. Heps me stay awake, ma'am."

Looking nervously at the little white box, I changed the subject. "How long will it be before we arrive in Savannah?" I hoped it wouldn't be one of those "long hauls" that required him to use what was in that little white box.

"I reckon we'll be thar purdy soon," he smiled.

An hour later, he drew up to the station. I offered to pay him but he wouldn't hear of it.

"Shur do like to hep some'n in trouble, ma'am. Don't you worry none about that van. I reckon that garage man's thar raht now." I thanked him kindly and breathed a sigh of relief as he waved goodbye.

The children stood on the sidewalk waving back until the semi disappeared from view.

"That was almost as much fun as Disney World," Pam giggled. "I can't wait to tell my friends. I bet a lot of them have never *seen* a truck that big."

"Let's go check on the train to Columbia," I said, shooing them into the station.

Fortunately, a train was leaving within an hour. I called to let Marlin know when we would arrive in Columbia. He met us at the station, happy that we had made it in time for their departure.

Back at the house, we related the tale of our latest adventure. Betty was concerned about her brother, but I told her not to worry.

"He's a big boy now and knows how to get around."

On that note, they left for their cruise to the Bahamas. After all, if anyone needed to worry about Bill, I could do that very well. At least he wasn't chuffing across the bay in a little boat. There's something comforting about living on dry land with trains and buses that run on schedule and never sink.

Just before dinner, a car drove into the driveway. Bill got out, paid the driver, and waved goodbye. We all ran to the door to hear his news. When everyone settled down, he began.

"The semi driver was right about the tow truck," he told us. "It arrived a half hour after you left. They couldn't fix the van there, so they towed it to a garage. It took a while, but they finally diagnosed a blown cylinder in the engine."

"Oh, my goodness. Can it be fixed?" I asked.

"Yes, but it's going to take a couple days to get parts and do the repairs. Instead of waiting around, I decided to hitchhike back here. In no time, I was picked up by a man heading north. He drove me right to the door. I gave him a few dollars for his time and petrol, and... here I am."

"Gosh!" Tia exclaimed. "We almost got left behind when the ship docked. We visited the Magic Kingdom. We broke down on the highway. We traveled in a semi truck. Dad had to hitch a ride home. And we've only been in America a few days!"

"Fair dinkum," Jackie said. "I wonder what the rest of our vacation will be like."

"It's going to be a beaut," Topper grinned.

"I can't wait to see what's next," Pam said dryly.

"I have an idea." Bill winked at me.

"What?" He had everyone's attention.

"Let's start the 'rest of our vacation' with dinner. I'm hungry."

*Chapter Fifteen*

# An Incredible Country

A week later, after a wonderful visit in South Carolina, we headed south again, this time to see my sister Goldie's family in Georgia. As an unexpected bonus, my sister June flew down from Michigan. Even though we looked older, we were still the same Goldie, June, and Connie. The three of us had not been together for seventeen years! It took a lot of talk to bridge that time span. We chatted non-stop for a week. Too soon, it was time to move on.

In Washington, D.C., we toured the inside of the White House.

"Just think," Bill told the children, "every president, except George Washington, has lived in this house. Imagine the great decisions that have been made within these walls during that time."

"Never mind the history," I said, looking up. "I want to know where they got those incredible chandeliers."

"They're so beautiful," Tia breathed, "just like America is beautiful."

Later, we took the elevator to the top of the Washington Monument. From each side, we looked out at a spectacular view. When we heard another tourist mention that President Nixon would soon be landing on the White House lawn, we rushed to the window on that side. Craning our necks, we were able to see the tiny figures gathering around a helicopter far below. The President of the United States emerged from the helicopter and walked across the White House lawn.

"Blimey!" Jackie exclaimed in awe. "Wait 'til my friends in school hear about this!"

"Too right," Pam breathed. She measured with her thumb and forefinger. "We've been this close to the President of the United States."

"That's something you'll never forget," their dad told them.

Next, we explored Mt. Vernon, the home of America's first president. The kids thought it was a lot more interesting than the White House.

"Look at this," Pam called from one of the bedrooms. "The bed is so high you have to use a ladder to go to bed at night."

"That's what that stool is for." Tia pointed to a step stool in the corner.

"I wouldn't want to fall out of that bed," Topper said solemnly.

Next, we visited Arlington National Cemetery, the last resting place for American service men and their families. We were just in time to see the changing of the guard at the Tomb of the Unknown Soldier. This tomb was erected to honor the memory of all American soldiers killed in battle who could not be identified. We sat on small bleachers to observe the solemn occasion as the sentries presented arms.

"What are they doing?" I whispered to Bill as they flipped their guns this way and that.

"They're performing maneuvers from the Army Manual of Arms," he whispered back without taking his eyes off the presentation.

At one of the quietest, most solemn moments, an eight-year-old voice piped up from the bleachers, "Can't those blokes figure out how to hold their guns?"

The people around us chuckled quietly. Red-faced, I leaned over and whispered to Topper, "I'll explain later. Be real quiet now."

In New Jersey, we visited the Badaraccos, our shipmates on the Monterey ten years ago. They were delighted to see us.

"My, the girls have grown," Flo exclaimed, "and still so pretty. I remember how their big brothers used to carry them around and the lovely dresses they wore."

"And this is the little Australian," Marty said, shaking Topper's hand. "Do you have any kangaroos on your farm?" he asked.

"No, sir, but we have wallabies. I saw a beaut one day. I almost snagged him, but he shot through into the woods and I lost him. I was ready to throw a willy."

"Well, well," Marty said, obviously confused by Topper's answer.

Bill took a moment to explain that wallabies are a miniature version of kangaroos.

"Topper almost caught one," he said, "but it ran off into the woods. Topper was about to have a fit."

"Ahh," Marty beamed, as it all became clear.

The next day, we crossed over to New York to visit Bill's cousin Jackie. I assured her that Aunt Jac was doing well.

"Skippy is taking good care of her while we're away."

Jackie lived in the Bronx. She told us she didn't go out at night without a siren and a police whistle.

"If you're around here about dark," she said, "you'll notice countless police appearing to take up their evening beats."

"Fair dinkum?" I asked. "Last night, we were driving around across the river in New Jersey. I was surprised at the number of people out walking dogs at eleven o'clock. Though I did notice that our friends had three locked doors between them and the street."

"New Jersey is a bit different than New York," Jackie sighed.

"Would you like to go to Battery Park?" Bill asked changing the subject. "We can ride on the subway."

The subway, usually famous for crowding, was half empty. Perhaps it was the cost. We paid eighteen dollars for six people to go five miles return. In comparison, a gallon of gas was twenty-nine cents.

I was appalled to see that the subway walls and cars had been spray-painted with names and slogans. This wanton vandalism gave me a chilly feeling of doom.

"Things got so bad," Jackie said, "our city government has banned the sale of spray paint."

"What has happened to America?" I cried.

The ferry crossing from Battery Park to the Statue of

Liberty raised my spirits. Although it stands on a base ten stories high, the statue itself was smaller than I thought it would be. A sign at the entrance warned us the climb to the statue's head was very arduous.

"Should we let the children go up?" I asked Bill.

"Of course," he said, "it's only twelve stories high."

Cousin Jackie didn't want to climb, so I waited with her on a lower level. We were chatting together when we heard a clattering on the stairs. I looked up and there was Bill followed by the children.

"Did you decide not to make the climb?" I asked when they jumped down the last few steps.

"No. We went up to the head. We had a great view from the top."

"How did you get up there so fast?"

Pam grinned, "We ran!"

"I beat everyone," Jackie boasted.

So much for warning signs. *Have Americans gone soft?* I wondered.

We went downstairs, under the statue, to a beautiful modern museum that had recently opened. Browsing through American history, I sensed the power that this nation once had. It was founded by men of different countries and became a haven for people of all lands. Like so many parents these days, I had to ask, "What went wrong? Did divorcing ourselves from the Bible have anything to do with these changes?"

That evening in downtown Jersey, we saw shop fronts secured with steel gates and doors. Many buildings had shop windows permanently bricked up. Some areas looked like a war zone.

"Ten years makes a lot of difference," Bill said, shaking his head.

The next day, on a brighter note, we drove through Connecticut to visit Bill's brother John and his wife, Norma. Jackie and Pam were delighted to find two girl cousins their ages to play with. Topper took a shine to a cat the size of a small dog. It did not like his attentions and became very adroit at escaping his grasp.

Although it was only September, the temperature suddenly dropped to twenty-six degrees. Norma treated us to an early Thanksgiving Dinner with real turkey. It was a nice change from our usual Thanksgiving duck in the summer heat of Australia. Topper found it strange.

"I reckon it's a bit cold for Thanksgiving," he opined, raising his eyebrows in surprise.

Before we left Connecticut, we wanted to show the children the place where I had lived while their dad was in the Philippines.

"I'm sure it was on this street," I said, as we cruised up and down. Finally, we questioned a passerby.

"Oh, yes," the stranger nodded, when we told him the address. "That's right by the new Sears store. Actually, it's their parking lot."

"Nothing ever stays put, does it?" I was disappointed.

In Massachusetts, we visited my brother Tim. Shivering with cold, I asked if there was a place where we could buy warm jackets.

"Yes," Carol said, "we have a brand new store called K-Mart. It's a whole new concept. They carry everything you could possibly want!"

She was right. The store was bigger than anything we

had ever seen. Bill and I walked around exclaiming over all the new gadgets. The kids kept calling, "Mom, Dad, come look at this!"

The store had clothes for all ages. With Carol guiding us, we bought quilted navy blue nylon jackets. They were warm enough for real cold weather, never wrinkled, and were perfect for stuffing into suitcases when the climate changed.

Cozy and warm in our new jackets, we drove on to Maine. In Portland, we stopped to visit Al and Gina Kunesh. Gina had been a neighbor and dear friend of my mother's when we lived in Rockland. We took the elevator to her apartment. No one was home.

Disappointed, we went back to the ground floor. As the elevator door opened, a lovely lady waiting in the lobby stood aside to let us out. I stopped. There was something familiar about her. We stared at each other.

"Connie!" she cried.

"Gina!" I exclaimed.

"I knew it was you!" she said. "You look just like your mother! Come on upstairs so we can visit." Another beautiful time spent with a dear friend.

After Portland, we drove on to Bath. The autumn foliage was breath-taking. We were getting closer to "home." We began to call out landmarks to the children.

"See the bridge we're coming to? It's the famous Bath bridge," Bill said.

As we started across, I pointed, "Look down there where those destroyers are. That's the Bath Iron Works. My uncle worked there during World War II. They built destroyers for the U.S. Navy."

Further on... "There's Moody's Diner! Our favorite place for hamburgers after the basketball and football games.

As we reached Rockland... "Look, there's the church I went to."

And a few minutes later... "That's where your mom grew up," Bill said, pointing to a white two-story house with dark green trim.

"Goodness," I said, "it seems much smaller now. See that big maple tree right beside the house?" They nodded. "I used to spend a lot of time climbing in that."

"Mom!" Tia laughed, "I can't imagine you climbing a tree!"

Jackie leaned over the seat. "Why don't you ever climb the eucalyptus tree with us?"

"Well, Jackie, I guess it's because I have so many other things to do," was my lame excuse. I crossed my fingers, hoping she wouldn't invite me to join her in their favorite tree when we went back to Australia.

Soon we were in Camden, where we visited Francis Eaton, Bill's boyhood pal and his wife, Elinor. The theme of the evening was, "Do you remember...?" One thing we all remembered was the taste of Down East lobsters.

"Can you guess what we're having for supper?" Elinor asked.

"It would have to be lobsters," Bill guessed. "You've never let us down on a visit yet."

He was right. A fresh boiled lobster appeared on every plate. The children were intrigued. Seeing their puzzled look, Francis demonstrated.

"This is how you do it. Use the nutcracker to break the hard shells and the little fork to dig the meat out. The rest you can do with your fingers."

"This is going to be fun," Jackie said, tackling the job.

"I always liked eating with my fingers," Tia admitted, "Now I'm allowed to do it!" She chuckled as she twisted one of the little claws open.

"What if I don't like lobster?" Pam was doubtful.

"Just give it to me, I'll eat it," Dad offered.

Happily dipping pieces of lobster into melted butter, we were told of the new American way of life.

"Yep," Francis twanged, "Gudda have a second television in every master bedroom, and a snowmobile or motor bike in every garage."

"Things sure have changed," Bill said, biting into a juicy piece of lobster. Wiping his chin, he added, "But lobster is still the same. Thank you, Elinor."

*Chapter Sixteen*

# Traveling On

We drove through New Hampshire, Vermont, and on to Montreal, Canada.

"This is where they opened *Expo 67* five years ago," Bill, our tour guide, explained. "From May to October that year, fifteen million people visited the Expo. Now they open a section each year. You'll be amazed at the Geodesic Dome. It's built from triangular panels with no internal support."

He was right. We were, indeed, amazed.

"Maybe we could build a house like that," Topper suggested, always looking for a better way. "Then we wouldn't have to chop down trees."

"I'm not sure we need anything that big," Tia observed dryly. "That's as big as a five-story building."

"We could make a little one." Topper wasn't willing to give up a good idea.

From Montreal, we followed the St. Lawrence River down to New York and camped at Niagara Falls. It was late in the afternoon and bitter cold.

"Let's get our chores done so we can go to the falls," I suggested.

Bill began to unload the camping gear. "Come on, Tia, let's get started on the tent." Their chore was the coldest, wettest job of all.

I called Topper. "Just get water from the tap now. Tomorrow you can sweep the van floor and get the boots clean. Pam, you and Jackie unpack the kitchen box. After dinner I'll help you with the dishes."

Everyone whisked through their chores and the meal. We wanted to be at the falls by dark to see the Illumination.

On the way to the falls, our "tour guide" explained, "Twenty thirty-six-inch searchlights create four billion, two hundred million candle-power to color the cataracts."

"How many candles?" Jackie squeaked in awe.

"Searchlights," Tia corrected. "They're as bright as that many candles."

"Oh," Jackie sighed, "I thought they were going to burn the place down."

The lights were spectacular. They played over the falls from the opposite bank, in an alternating blue and rose light-pattern, turning the cataracts into hues of purple, green, red, blue, and yellow.

"It's like fairyland," Jackie cooed.

"Wait till my teacher hears about this." Pam was awestruck.

The next day, we went down the trail into the gorge.

"Look at that boat," Topper called. "What's it doing

way down here?"

"That's a steamer," his dad explained. "*The Maid of the Mist* takes visitors around the river at the base of the falls."

"That's a good name for it," Tia noted. "There's plenty of mist down here."

"Let's go back up before we get soaked," Pam suggested, pulling her jacket tightly around her.

Curious, I counted the steps going up from the gorge. There were 325, "puff, puff, puff."

"What's next?" I asked Bill, hoping for a chance to sit.

"The elevator," he said. "It goes to the bottom of the falls and then up to the tower. From there we can see both the American and Canadian sides at the same time."

"Two countries at once!" Jackie said in surprise. "You've got to be kidding."

"That will save us lots of time," Pam concluded.

"Sounds good to me," her dad agreed, thinking of the next leg of our trip.

From the tower, we saw the American Falls and a bridge.

"That's Canada just on the other side of the bridge that joins the two countries," Dad explained. "We'll be crossing it tomorrow."

"Fair dinkum," I said, "another country and we don't have to go by boat!"

After the thrill of Niagara, we traveled on. Entering Michigan at Detroit, we had a rude awakening. The drivers were crazy. The highways were littered with debris from accidents. But visiting June, Don, and their eight children in Kalamazoo made up for the road madness.

The children had a great time with their cousins. Big families are terrific. After a traditional "family dinner," we spent a delightful evening having a "family sing" around the fireplace. I felt sorry for the people of this age. They've been convinced that if they have more than two children, the world will become overpopulated. Watching the happy faces around me, I was glad that we had ignored those voices of doom.

One morning, the children were playing together in the basement when something rolled under the washing machine.

"Go get a torch," Tia told Topper as they tried to fish it out.

"No!" their cousins shouted in alarm. "You'll burn the house down!"

"It's all right," I calmed them. They eyed me strangely. "A torch is just a flashlight," I explained.

Even with the language barrier, we had a wonderful time. Just before we left, the weather treated us to a small snowstorm. It was a brand new experience for the Moore children. It was mid-October. The newspapers hailed it as the earliest snowstorm in 103 years—another weather record to add to our collection. While we were packing up, the kids scooped up enough snow to fill our cooler—a souvenir from Kalamazoo that lasted for days.

As we passed through Illinois and Iowa, temperatures were down in the twenties and forties. Most campsites were empty. One morning, our telescoping tent poles were frozen open. Tia took them to the ladies room to thaw them under hot water.

"That's the only way I could retract the poles to get the tent packed up," she said.

It was drizzling in South Dakota. But fortunately, the weather cleared enough for us to see the carvings on Mt. Rushmore.

"America is truly an incredible country," I sighed as Bill and I gazed up at the carvings. "Each state has its own awesome scenery."

"And we're only half way around," he reported. "There are still a lot of wonders to behold."

In Wyoming, we stopped to let the children roll in the snow and make snowballs.

"Snow is cold, but snow is fun," Topper shouted, lobbing a snowball at Jackie.

"Watch it!" she yelled back with some ammunition of her own. I stopped what might have been a mini war by asking them if they knew how to make snow angels.

"Snow what?" Pam wanted to know.

"You lay down in the snow," I directed, "put your arms above your head. Then move them down past your sides patting the snow down as you do. Spread your feet and do the same thing." I waited till they finished. "Now stand up and look. What do you see?"

"Snow angels!" they cried in unison.

At Yellow Stone National Park, they discovered more winter fun. In their boots, they "skated" along the icy boardwalks all around the geyser, waiting for it to erupt. Within five minutes of the estimated time, Old Faithful shot a steaming water-geyser 120 feet into the air. Old Faithful hasn't failed in over a hundred years we were told.

Moving on to Washington state, we visited the Fergursons who lived in sugar beet country. We talked about Rusty's time with them.

"He's due back in the States soon," Bill told them. "We hope he'll arrive before we have to return to Australia. It would be wonderful to see him again."

"Do you still have horses, Mr. Fergurson?" Jackie was bold enough to ask.

"Sure," he said. "Want to ride one?" There was no doubt about the answer to that question. While Ruth and I visited, Bill and Dick took the children out to ride the horses. They were thrilled.

After a few days of fun on the farm, we were back on the trail, winding our way along the Oregon coast. We curved up and down through the mist-shrouded mountains and around rocky cliffs, above the pounding, churning ocean.

Unnerved by the buffeting wind, I pleaded for a more inland route. Bill obliged. It was still up and down mountains, but not as windy.

In Northern California, we passed through the Redwood Forest. We were all agog at the size of the pine trees. At one stop, Tia, Pam, Jackie, and Topper, with arms outstretched, tried to circle one of the trees but could barely make it halfway around.

"Daddy," Tia asked our on-site tour guide, "how do these trees grow so big?"

"Well," he said importantly, "the deep protected folds of Northern California's coastal range, with ocean breezes and crisp, cool fogs drifting inland, combine to make ideal climatic conditions for their growth."

"Fair dinkum," I said, "how do you know all that?"

"I just read it in this little book." He grinned, and read on. "Oh, the wonders of nature. The Redwoods are California's own special treasure. These pine trees mature at 200 feet with a diameter of ten feet. But that's only a start. Some are over 300 feet and still growing."

Later we came to a split in the road. Part went around a huge Redwood and part went right through the tree. Though still living and growing, the tree had been hollowed-out for traffic.

"Daddy," Topper yelled, "we can drive through the tree!"

Unfortunately, as we drew nearer, we noticed a sign cautioning high vehicles to go around the tree.

"That's crook," Pam moaned, "our van is too tall."

Refusing to miss out on a lifetime experience, Jackie asked, "Why can't we get out and walk through?"

"Jolly good idea," I applauded. Bill parked the van off the road, and with great satisfaction, we all walked through the opening and back again.

"Not everybody gets to walk through a tree," Tia said, climbing into the van.

"And we did it twice!" Topper crowed.

Back on the highway, we wended our way down to Southern California and warmer weather. We visited Universal Studios where everything was a movie prop. We took pictures of the girls in jail. And one of Topper, the strong man, lifting a boulder bigger than he was. It looked like the real thing, but it was only cleverly painted Styrofoam.

"Now we know a bit more about how fake movies are," Tia summed it up.

In Arizona, the desert is hardly what you would expect. It teems with life and growth of the most unusual kind. The Saguaro Cactus grows in interesting shapes, looking like people with their arms in different positions. It kept us entertained, trying to imagine what attitude they were portraying. Were they mad, sad, singing, or pointing?

From the desert floor, and sweater weather, we climbed four thousand feet to Flagstaff. It didn't seem that high because the tops of the mountains were flat. We traveled from mesa to mesa, harried by dangerous crosswinds. We stayed in motels each night, but they were hard to find.

Finally, we descended to a milder climate of rolling hills and grazing cattle, but not for long. Leaving warm sunny skies behind, we met blustery snow in Texas.

"Oh, no," Tia moaned, looking at the white landscape, "our tent posts will freeze again!"

"You're right," Bill said. "There's too much snow to set up camp." It was mid-November. We found a motel for the night and called my sister in Georgia.

"Hi, how would you like to have company for Thanksgiving?" She was delighted.

With that goal in mind, we scooted through Oklahoma and hurried on through Arkansas. We arrived in Georgia just in time for Thanksgiving. Over a wonderful feast, Goldie and Robbie were full of questions about our trip. That was a good thing because the children had plenty of tales to tell.

After we settled down, Bill checked with Betty in South Carolina. She had wonderful news! Rusty was on his way back from Vietnam!

"I told her we'll start back tomorrow," Bill said, apologizing to Goldie and Robbie. "Sorry we need to leave so soon, but we want to be there when he arrives."

"Of course you do," Goldie said with understanding. They were as excited as we were. The following morning, after a heart-warming breakfast, they accepted our grateful thanks for their hospitality and wished us God-speed.

*Chapter Seventeen*

# Unexpected Events

Heading for South Carolina, I began to reflect on all the wonderful friends we had visited and all the memories we had built together over the years. I wondered about Rusty. He had served his country well and survived the Vietnam war. What were his plans for the future? He would finish his enlistment in the States, but what would he do after that? Would he choose to live here or in Australia?

As soon as the children had settled down and were preoccupied with their studies, I looked at Bill.

"Hon." Immediately, I had his attention. Hon is the universal code word for "watch out, your wife has another bright idea."

He glanced at me, "What?"

"Do you think it would be wise for us to move back to the States?" I hurried on before he could answer. "We've already planned to leave the island and would be saying goodbye to the farm anyway."

To my surprise, he answered quietly, "I wouldn't mind at all. My mother is getting older. She is very distressed because we live so far away. Betty has wanted us to come back for a long time. And you need to be closer to your family."

"True, but I'm concerned about the children. We don't know whether Rusty will stay here when his time is up, or want to go back to Australia. If he does stay, how long will it be before some of the others decide to join him? Mickey would be tempted by all the modern improvements here. Skippy would come back just for the adventure of doing it. I'm not sure about Topper and the girls. Their friends are on the mainland, but they haven't had the opportunity to become really close yet. Fortunately, they do seem to like it in the States."

"I understand," he sighed. "We could end up with half the family here and the other half thousands of miles away." He thought for a while then asked, "What would we do with the land and buildings we have left?"

"We could divide the land into blocks with the house on one of them. Bernie Ryan does that kind of surveying work."

"What about Aunt Jac?"

"Oh goodness, I don't know. Would she want to move again? That's going to be a tough one."

"Well, we'll see," he said, ending the conversation. I smiled, thinking of Bill's motto: *Don't worry unless you have to.*

When we arrived at Betty's house, she ran out with the news as soon as she heard the van.

"Rusty will be back in early December! You can stay, can't you?" she pleaded.

"Yes, if you don't mind," Bill said. "We would love to stay long enough to spend some time with him."

"The travel trailer is all yours," Marlin offered. "Actually, we bought it in case you wanted to stay for a while. I'll help you get settled."

We set up housekeeping in the nineteen-foot trailer. It was a cozy home away from home. The children busied themselves playing with Jani, entertaining Grandmother Moore, and catching up on their school work.

When Rusty phoned to say he was on his way, Betty rushed out to give us the good news.

"He'll be here tomorrow," she announced. "I didn't tell him you were here. It will be fun to surprise him."

"Who's coming?" Topper asked, hearing all the excitement.

"Your brother," Uncle Marlin told him. "Go find the girls and tell them the good news."

As girls do, they began to make plans. What to wear, how to decorate the table, and could Aunt Betty cook his favorite dinner? It was hard to go to bed that night and even more difficult to go to sleep.

Morning came with great anticipation. The children sailed through their chores and prepared for the big event.

"Do you think he'll be surprised to see us here?" Jackie asked.

"Do you think he will have his uniform on?" Pam wanted to know.

"Of course he will," Tia assured them on both counts.

We did surprise him! He had no idea that we were still in the States. As we talked into the evening hours, it was apparent that Rusty, as well as other Vietnam vets, had suffered deep trauma and pain. From the war, yes, but even more so from the way the American government had treated its troops.

"When the war was winding down," he told us after the children had gone to bed, "they took away our guns and put them in the armory. When the Viet Cong attacked, we had to run and get them before we could defend ourselves. A lot of guys didn't make it," he finished in a muffled voice, staring into the distance.

"I'm deeply sorry," I told him, putting my arms around him. "We're so thankful God brought you back safely. And thankful that we could be together for a while. By the way, Dad and I have been talking about moving back to the States."

"Really?" he said, his face brightening. "That would be great. I like Australia, but I feel my future is here. What do the other kids think of the idea?"

"They don't know yet. We've just started talking about it ourselves. But I really don't think they would mind, since we were planning to move off the island anyway."

"I wouldn't mind," Tia said, appearing on the scene.

"Nothing is sure yet," I cautioned her, "so it's best not to say anything to the girls and Topper."

"Yes, ma'am, I won't," she assured me, "but I do like it here."

"That's two of us," Rusty grinned.

When his leave was up, he was scheduled to report to Fort Ord in California. But Marlin, an army man himself, told Rusty he could get an early release. He was able to do that and enrolled in a flight training school in Tulsa, Oklahoma, under the GI Bill.

"This time," he said, "I'm going to learn to fly fixed-wing planes. I've had enough of helicopters for a while."

With that good news, we said our goodbyes and headed for Charleston. We wanted to return to Australia via Europe and were hoping to fly Military Air Transport. When he was in the Navy, Bill had tried to get stationed in Europe many times, but was always sent back to the Pacific area. Since we had never been to that part of the world, we thought this would be a good opportunity to visit another culture.

Unfortunately, it was so close to Christmas all the seats were taken by soldiers going home on leave. After a couple of days, we realized that "space available" was not going to work. Finally, Bill made a hard decision.

"Europe will have to wait for another day. It's time for us to go home."

We flew back to Australia for a lot more money than it cost for our three-week tour aboard ship.

Just hours from cold South Carolina, we landed in Sydney. It was a super-hot, hundred degree plus, Australian summer. We walked down the plane's steps and crossed the tarmack.

"I feel like I'm going to burn up," Tia complained. "How could it get so hot, so quick?"

"Good thing we packed away our winter jackets," Pam observed. "We sure won't need them here."

"No more snow angels," Jackie said sadly.

"But we get to swim in our own pool," said Topper, looking at the bright side.

## Tell Australia Goodbye? You've Got to be Kidding!

Bill called home to arrange for Skippy to pick us up when we reached Brisbane.

"Skippy isn't at home," Aunt Jac told him. "He's taken some friends to the Gold Coast for the weekend."

Disappointed, we flew on to Brisbane. When we landed, Bill rang Mr. Jackson and arranged for him to pick us up at Redland Bay. Sorry that we had missed Skippy, we rented a station wagon, stuffed our twenty pieces of luggage in, and headed for home.

"I can see Mr. Jackson's boat waiting," Tia said as we approached the jetty. "I'll be so glad to get back to my own room and my own bed."

"I'll help load the luggage onto the trolley," Bill said. "Then you roll it out to the boat while I park the station wagon. I'll take it back to Brisbane tomorrow." We shifted everything on to the trolley and pushed it to the end of the jetty.

"G'day!" Mr. Jackson greeted us. "Jolly good to have you back," he said, as we handed him the luggage.

"As we passed bag after bag onto the boat, Pam groaned, "I'd almost forgotten what it's like to live on an island."

Just as we finished loading, Bill arrived carrying bits and pieces that we had left behind in the car. He hailed Mr. Jackson and climbed aboard.

"How are you going to get all those suitcases to your house when we reach the island?" Mr. Jackson asked.

"I'm not sure," Bill replied, shaking his head.

"If you want," Mr. Jackson offered, "I'll take you around to my jetty. We can use my lorry. It's big enough to hold the lot."

Thankful, Bill agreed. At Jacksonville, we unloaded everything from the boat and toted it along the jetty to the truck. Still dressed in our best traveling clothes, we climbed up beside the luggage. After five months of easy living in the States, we arrived home three days before Christmas, hot and sweaty, on the back of a dusty lorry.

"Welcome to Russell Island," I murmured.

Aunt Jac met us at the door. All smiles to see us home? No. Her first words were, "I have made arrangements to fly back to the States in January."

"That's wonderful," I said, remembering the luxury we had just left behind. My second thought was, why did she feel she had to make that decision without letting us know first?

Later, we learned that she and Skippy had not seen eye to eye. She wanted to pamper him. He did not want to be pampered. She wanted him to pamper her. Unfortunately, pampering is not a Moore trait. They were not the happy duo I had envisioned when we left.

"Oh well," I sighed. "Back to the real world. Merry Christmas," I muttered to the door, as I dragged my suitcase through.

*Chapter Eighteen*

# Our Family Gets Smaller

Skippy was stunned to see us when he got back from the Gold Coast.

"I thought you were going to Europe! What happened? How did you get home?"

Dad told him how we had gotten to Fiddler's Green from the airport and why, for the present, we had passed up Europe.

"I guess it was a good thing," he reasoned, "because if we had made the trip to Europe, Aunt Jac wouldn't have been here when we got back."

"Too right," Skippy said. "I couldn't be home all the time and when I was here, I had plenty to do taking care of the farm and preparing to sit for my Senior Exams. Aunt Jac was lonely. Five months with the family away was a long time. Especially when her friends were busy with other things."

Australia had been a difficult transition for Aunt Jac. Before she came, we thought we had covered every possibility for anxiety or distress. We missed one. The hemisphere. There is a complete "upside-down-ness" when you move from one hemisphere to another.

For over forty years, Aunt Jac had lived in rural Maine. Her house was nestled next to a forest of pine trees. She fed the birds and deer from the woods during winter snows or when their food was scarce.

"I put their food out before I fed myself," she told me. "They would be waiting by the door for me to wake up. I just couldn't enjoy eating if I knew they were hungry."

She had planted her gardens in the spring and harvested them in the fall. The sky, rather than the radio, told her what the weather was going to be. The stars guided her at night. She knew the constellations and where to find them at different times of the year.

"It's not the same in the Southern Hemisphere," she said wistfully. "The sky changes when you're down under. I guess that's why I feel so confused and disoriented."

When she tried to read the sky, it would not give her the right answers. The summer sky was now a winter sky and the winter sky summer. I sympathized with her. We had been through the same difficult transition. During our first years in Australia, our biological clocks urged us to harvest when everyone else was planting, and to plant when everyone else was harvesting.

With the older boys away, there just wasn't enough time for the attention Aunt Jac craved. The girls and Topper were at school and Bill worked on the mainland. I was the only farmer left. Up in the fields plowing with the tractor or scuffling with the hoe, I'd hear Aunt Jac yoo-hooing from

## Our Family Gets Smaller

down in the yard. Thinking something was wrong, I'd stop everything and rush to meet her. Waving two spools of thread above her head, she would call, "Which color should I use on the dress you want me to mend?"

Bill and I had discussed the problem during our evening walks. We were hoping it would be better for her when we moved to the mainland. Before we left for our vacation in the States, we hunted for a house with a little apartment for her but were unable to find one. We were considering having a home built that would accommodate all of us.

I was relishing the idea of a lovely brick home at Redland Bay on the "other" side of the water. It sounded like heaven to me. I had long ago discovered that I am not an island person. I love the idea of getting into my car and driving to the store, schools, or library. Our time in the States reminded me of that almost forgotten luxury. That's why I was happy for Aunt Jac when she said she was going back home.

The next issue of "The Islander" carried the news:

*Mrs. Mary Bragdon, who has become well known on Russell Island, leaves for her home in Morrell, Maine, U.S.A., on January 18th. While in Australia, she has been the guest of Mr. and Mrs. Bill Moore of Russell Island. Residents of the island said farewell to Mrs. Bragdon at a send-off party in the Public Hall last Thursday. She will be missed by her many newly-made friends.*

She will also be missed by the Moore family. We had built precious memories in our three years together at Fiddler's Green.

"I'm going to miss Aunt Jac," Pam said. "She used to pay me a dime to clean her room and do errands."

"I'll miss her too," Jackie grinned. "She used to bang on the pipes when we made too much noise upstairs."

"She gave me cookies," Topper sighed.

"She taught me lots of sewing tricks," Tia said wistfully.

"It's all happened so quick," I told Bill. "Almost before we've had time to unpack from our trip, we're saying bye to Aunt Jac. The grandmother we had always wanted is leaving us."

"I know," he said with sympathy. "She told me she is eighty-six years old and felt that it was getting close to her time to die. When that happened, she wanted to be in the land where she was born."

"Well, there is one good thing about this situation," I declared.

"What's that?" Bill asked.

"Your cousin has moved back to Maine and will be able to take care of Aunt Jac."

"Yes, that is a good thing," he agreed.

Feeling better, knowing that she would be well cared for, we helped her pack her antique steamer trunk. Bill sent it over on the barge. It would follow her to the States. When it was time for her flight, we all met in the yard to say our goodbyes. It was there in the yard we had welcomed her three and a half years ago.

Bill loaded her suitcase into the trunk and helped her into the car. We waved our last goodbye as they drove off to the jetty. Bill would be staying with her until she was safely settled on the plane. As I watched the car disappear out of sight, I could feel the chill winds of change begin to

## Our Family Gets Smaller

blow into our lives once more. Aunt Jac was no longer with us and Skippy had finished his senior year in December.

Bill returned the next day with a good report. Aunt Jac was happily on her way. He had called his cousin in Maine who promised she would be there to meet her when the plane landed.

That evening, for the first time since we had arrived home, we went for a walk under the stars.

"I wonder if Aunt Jac will be happy to see her familiar Northern Hemisphere sky," I mused, looking up at the new moon.

"I don't know," he said, "but when we talked about moving back to the States, Aunt Jac was our biggest question mark. Now what do you think?"

"I remember you saying, 'We'll see.' You were right not to waste time worrying. It has all happened for the best. I think it's time we talked to Skippy first and then the younger ones. Skippy has been busy catching up on farm chores since he left school. But now that you're back to take care of things, he's anxious to take that next step."

"Let's do that when we get home," Bill suggested.

We finished our walk and climbed the stairs. Skippy was reading and the others were asleep. The three of us sat down to talk over a cup of tea and cookies.

"Are you still planning to go to Mackay?" I asked, passing the plate of date nut squares.

"Mmmm," he sighed, biting into a cookie. "I really missed these while you were gone." He chewed a bit, then offered, "If you don't need me here, I'd like to give it a go. Uncle Tom says he can get me a job with another surveying crew in Mackay. Mickey's doing well up there. I think I could too."

"That's a good start," his dad said, "but I think you should know we've been talking about moving back to the States."

"Fair dinkum?" His eyebrows shot up. "You've got to be kidding! I thought you were moving to the mainland."

"We were, but things have changed," Dad explained. "My mother is not doing well. She was very distressed to see us leave again. Then, there are our brothers and sisters and their families. But most of all, Rusty wants to stay in the States. I don't blame him, there is a lot available for him there. But somehow, I have a feeling that you and Mickey would soon follow, and then we'd have children on two continents. Since we are going to move anyway, it seems prudent to try to keep the family together."

"It won't be right away," I cautioned. "There is time for us all to think it over and decide what's best for everyone."

Listening to them chat about the pros and cons of the idea, I smiled wistfully. Our boys had grown up. We would be leaving our island farm. The future was an empty page, waiting to be written upon.

*Chapter Nineteen*

# Making Plans

With less to do on the farm, Topper and the girls began to explore the island.

Packing lunches, they spent hours roaming the woods and beaches. No doubt they had lots of adventures. Though I'm not sure I want to know what they were. Probably the kind I never told my mom about because I knew what she would say: "That's dangerous, Connie, you had better stay around the house where it's safe."

Too soon, it was time for a new school year. The children had finished their grades by Correspondence School during our travels. It was easy for them to slide into their new classes when school started. They traveled on Noyes' boat with their dad. He had found a job working heavy equipment at Redland Bay. With all the big brothers gone, Bill was on hand to drive them to and from the jetty.

Tia was the first to notice a big difference. "I wish we didn't have to go by boat all the time," she fussed, coming up the steps. "I liked it better in the States."

"Me too," Pam chimed in. "When are we going to move to the Mainland?" she asked when she saw me at the door.

"Yes," Jackie added just behind her. "We would have been home a long time ago if we didn't have to come by boat."

"It is a long day," I agreed. "Put your things away and eat your snack. Do your chores, and we'll talk about moving at dinner."

When they had gone their separate ways, I refilled the teacups and sat down with Bill.

"What do you think?" I asked. "Should we tell them now?"

"Well, the boys agree, you and I agree, and they seem to be agreeable. Let's tell them and go on from there."

"When are we moving?" Topper asked at dinner as soon as his tummy was full. He had not forgotten my promise.

I looked at Bill. He nodded for me to go ahead.

"How would you like to move back to the States?" I asked, jumping in with both feet.

"I'd love to!" Jackie said.

"Another adventure," Topper declared.

Pam was surprised. "Fair dinkum?" she asked, looking at me round-eyed.

"What about Mickey and Skippy?" Tia said slowly, with a worried look.

"They'll be going with us. Rusty has already decided to stay in the States," Dad explained. "We just wanted to talk it over with you before we make our final decision."

"Where would we live?" practical Pam asked. "Close to Grandma and Aunt Betty?"

Dad smiled. "As close as we can," he said.

"Goodie!" Topper was ready. "Let's go!"

"When would we leave?" Jackie wondered.

"It will be quite a few months," Dad explained. "We have a lot of things to take care of first."

By the end of February, Bernie Ryan, the surveyor, had drawn up plans to subdivide the two acres into six blocks.

"You will need a road along here," he said, pointing to a line on the diagram. "Would you like to choose a name for the road?"

"Yes," I said, winking at Bill, "let's call it American Avenue." He grinned and nodded to Bernie. Four blocks were to be listed on the market. We kept the other two with the house. We were slowly cutting our ties to Russell Island.

With that settled, Bill gathered his maps and began working on our trip back to the States.

One Sunday after breakfast, he asked, "Want to see what I've planned?"

"I'd love to. How about going to the gazebo where it's quiet? I'll fix our coffee while you get your things together."

Balancing maps and coffee cups, we climbed up into the gazebo and settled down.

"Are we finally going to get to Europe?" I asked.

"Righto! I've booked passage on the *Galileo Galilao* for June. That's an Italian ship…"

"Well, I hope it's better than the *Australis*. That ship was built in 1940 and still had the same engines!"

"I remember that," Bill grinned. "They were always belching clouds of black smoke. Sometimes we wondered if we were going to make it to the States."

"Too right. When you and the children got sick, I thought it was seasickness and prescribed fresh air and exercise."

"Didn't work, did it?" Bill winced at the memory.

"No, but when I found out there was a gastro epidemic aboard, I changed the treatment to bed rest and lots of vitamin C. Everyone improved rapidly after that. Sorry, didn't mean to interrupt you."

"That's all right. The Greek ship was pretty bad. I'm sure the Italian one will be better. Now, back to our itinerary. We'll sail from Sydney and stop at Melbourne and Perth before going around the African horn to Capetown."

"That's nice. I'd like to see Melbourne and Perth again. Capetown should be interesting too. I've read stories about going around 'the horn' and now I'm actually going to do it."

"From there," Bill continued, "our next port will be the Canary Islands. You'll love that stop. I've read it's a beautiful place. A lot of tourists go there. After that, we'll sail through the straits of Gibraltar and stop at Malta, Greece, and Sicily…"

"Europe at last!" I cried, clapping my hands.

"Righto, our last port will be in Italy. We'll debark in Naples for the next leg of our journey."

"Sounds exciting. You've done a good job."

"Thanks. By the way, I've registered us with the Youth Hostels Association."

"What's that?"

"Mostly for young people, it's an organization that offers basic accommodations at very low cost. You get a bed, clean linens, and sometimes a meal. Occasionally, you're expected to lend a hand with the chores. Hostels are very regulated and demand good behavior."

"But we're not young people."

"They do allow families in some hostels. We'll just have to pick and choose. I like the idea because we'll see more of each country and perhaps get to understand the people better."

"Jolly good, what's next?"

"I'm going to buy Euro Passes for train travel."

"What are they?"

"They allow us to get off and on trains that fit in with our schedule. We can travel from Naples to Holland that way."

"We can stop anywhere we want to?"

"Yes. We'll hostel all the way through Austria, Switzerland, Germany, France, Belgium, and Holland."

"Wow, that's a lot of traveling, but then, we've always wanted to see Europe. What happens after Holland?"

"Then we'll take a ferry across to Dover and on to London. Wendy lives there. We'll be able to visit her and see the sights."

"Jolly good! It will be wonderful to see Wendy, Maureen, and Chris again. They were so nice to us when we first came to Australia. It's because of them we decided to leave Perth and come to Queensland. Gosh, that was a long time ago..." My voice trailed off as memories played through my mind. Bill sipped his coffee waiting for me to return to the present.

"Do you think we'll ever stay in one place for long?" I wondered.

"Probably not," my adventurer replied. "Want to know what's next?"

"I'm already overwhelmed, but tell me anyway."

"For the third leg of our journey, I've scheduled us on a Protea Small-Bus Camping Tour from London."

"What's a Camping Tour?"

"It's a small bus that holds ten people with tents and camping gear."

"You mean we'll be going on a camping trip without having to carry our own tents and gear?"

"Yes," he grinned. "Quite a concept, isn't it?"

"Righto, where will this tour take us?"

He traced a line on the map with his finger. "From London, we'll take the ferry back to Holland. Then we go through northern Germany and on to Denmark, Sweden, and Norway. We'll finish the tour back in Newcastle, England."

"Now I'm really overwhelmed," I laughed. "I hope that's all."

"Yes, that's the end of the camping tour." He folded up his map and reached for another. "But... there's a bit more," he added. "You'll like this part. Remember we've always wanted to go to Ireland where our families came from?"

"Fair dinkum! Are we going to Ireland?"

"Too right," he smiled at my excitement. "From Newcastle, we'll go by train to Scotland, then back through England and Wales."

"What happened to Ireland?" I was confused.

Patiently, he explained, "We have to take a ferry from Wales across the Irish Sea to get to Ireland."

"Oh," I marveled, "I'm glad you know where we're going. I'd get lost for sure. Now what do we do next? Go home?"

"Not quite," he said thoughtfully. "I think we should go back to London to recoup before we fly to South Carolina."

"Jolly good," I sighed. "After all that, a little rest will be just the thing. By the way, how long will this wonderful journey take?"

"Three or four months," he said, folding up his maps. I was speechless.

"One more thing," he said, helping me down from the gazebo. "Let's ask Rusty if he could join us on the trip."

I wrote to Rusty who was still in Flight Training School in Tulsa, Oklahoma. "Would it be possible for you to join us in Europe for a while?"

He wrote back, "I'm sorry I can't make it, but I have some very good news. I was at the top of my class in my instrument instructor test. I'm preparing now for my check ride and multi-engine training."

Between classes, he planned to visit his aunts (my sisters) in Michigan and Missouri. We cheered that decision. Ever since he had gone back to the States, we hoped he would be able to visit family. I wanted my brother and sisters to get acquainted with Rusty as an adult.

Soon after that, an unusual letter came in the mail. It was from Mrs. Johnson who lived in Tulsa, Oklahoma. She wrote using Rusty's stateside nickname, "Bill":

*Dear Mrs. Moore,*

*You and I have never met, but my husband and I do know your son Bill— and it is about him that I am writing. We met Bill through our nephew, who is also a student at the Ross Aviation Flying School here in Tulsa.*

*After the initial meeting, Bill would drop over to visit with us on numerous occasions. He told us of his life in Australia and his overseas tour in Vietnam—and he made it all very interesting! I might add, he pitched in and helped my husband paint the trim on our house and plant bushes, and is most willing to be of help.*

*You and your husband have raised a son you can take pride in. I find him quite mature for his age and a very likable young man.*

My heart was touched—first by her kindness in taking time to write, and even more so, I was thankful for answered prayers. I have always enlisted God's help to develop my children into people who would be a credit to Him. I've never tried to make them fit into a mold that I had created, but always encouraged them to do their very best with the talents they had been given.

*Chapter Twenty*

# Going Home

We had just five months left to work out what we would take with us—and what had to be left behind.

"We have some big decisions to make," Bill said one morning after breakfast. "I've ordered a dozen three-by-four-foot wooden crates to ship our things back to the States. We can only take what will fit into those crates."

"Goodness," I was surprised. "Do you remember when our shipment came over from the States?"

"Sure do," he acknowledged. "A truck arrived with six overseas crates. Each one the size of a small room."

"And now," I scolded, "you expect me to get everything into twelve small crates just three feet by four feet."

"Well," he said, "do you really want to pay to send our old furniture back? Or appliances that won't run on Stateside electricity? Wouldn't it be better to buy new when we get there?"

"Well put," I said, pulling in my horns. "That makes sense. I'm sorry I didn't think of it that way."

We agreed to keep about a hundred books from our 500-volume library. We added dishes, crystal, silverware, linens, and tools. We saved room for our most precious possessions—the children's early school papers, costumes, Japanese kimonos, and other irreplaceable "stuff."

There were two things I hated to part with. One was a beautiful paint-by-number oil of the Red Shoes Ballet. I had painted the graceful ballerina picture years ago when we lived in Brunswick, Maine. It looked elegant on any wall in the frame Bill had made for it. Sadly, it was too large to fit into a crate. The other treasure was an Australian silky oak end table. I loved both items because they spoke of beauty.

We introduced a new American custom to Russell Island—yard sales. We had one almost every weekend. Strangely, Lucy Porter was one of our biggest buyers. I wondered if she was shopping for herself or for others.

"Perhaps this is our legacy to Russell Island," I mused, as I watched our possessions disappear one by one.

Bill arranged for Gerard to stay on as caretaker until the house was sold. He happily settled into Aunt Jac's vacated room. Mickey and Skippy came down from Mackay to help, bringing their belongings with them.

With everything taken care of, we gathered around the table one more time for our last meal together at Fiddler's Green. It was a sad time. It was a happy time.

After dinner, I read a letter that had arrived in the mail. "It's from Mrs. Sliep," I announced.

"Oh," Tia was surprised. "She was my favorite Easter grandmother."

"That's right," Mickey said. I saw her at the nursing home in Redland Bay. She's doing very well for a widow in her 80s. What did she say?"

I read the letter:

*Dear Connie and all the family,*

*Thank you for your very nice card, every one of you. I should have written before but I did not know whether you were home. And there was a rumor that you had sold out and come to live on the mainland. So I did not know where to write.*

*It's lovely to be you, to go traveling about everywhere. And now I am going to lose a very dear family. In fact, the only nice family on the Island, and that's the truth. Give my love to the girls. I remember them in their pretty little frocks with large sashes from a long time ago. Also the dear boys, every one of them. One used to carry his baby brother on his back in a little carry-all. A most beautiful sight to remember.*

*I have a photo of Bill and the boys and girls but not one of you. If you have one, I would like it very much to remember a nice and dear family. I wish you success wherever you may be and hope the change will be for your happiness. My love to every one of you.*

*Marjory Sliep*

"That makes me sad," tender-hearted Jackie said.

"I know." I reached out to give her a hug. "We've done so

many things and met so many wonderful people here. Sometimes it was hard, but then, we did have a lot of fun too."

"Mom," Mickey, the thinker of deep thoughts said, "things were pretty lean when we first moved here, but even as kids we weren't discouraged. There was a lot of work to do and a lot of island to explore. We were good workers and very progressive too. You and Dad were determined to build a future for us kids."

Tears welled up in my eyes as he went on.

"The experiences we've had on the island and the farm have made us independent. We learned to be creative. When something on the farm needed to be fixed, improved, or built better, we did it! You and Dad made a unique empire from the neglected farm that was here when we came."

I smiled at him. Mickey had a way of lifting spirits.

Tia picked up the theme. "That's right, Mom. We're leaving behind the best house on the island. No one else has a bathroom upstairs and a shower downstairs."

"Righto," Skippy continued. "We planted an orchard and made a tennis court. We built the cement steps leading down to the pool. We made a concrete apron around the pool. We constructed built-in planters and the retaining walls, all with blocks we made ourselves."

Gerard had his opinion too. "No one has mentioned the laundry, rumpus room, the new workshop, or the storage buildings. All very important," he grinned.

"Don't forget the flowers, Mom," Jackie said. catching the spirit. "You and Mickey worked out gardens full of beautiful flowers all around the house." She finished on a wistful note, with downcast eyes, "I'm going to miss making bouquets for the table," she said quietly.

## Going Home

"I'm going to miss the woods and beaches," Topper said.

"I'm going to miss this beautiful six-bedroom home," I declared.

"Well, there's something I already miss," Bill said.

"What's that?" we all wanted to know.

"My dessert," he said. "We haven't had our ice cream yet."

"Oh, Daddy!" Pam said, heading for the kitchen.

Last goodbyes were difficult. The day we left, Gerard drove us to the jetty one last time. He helped us load the luggage onto the trolley. One last time, we pushed the trolley along its rails. One last time, we passed everything across to be stowed on Mr. Jackson's boat. That was it. Everything was done. It was time for one last goodbye.

"Hey! Where's Skippy?" Mickey asked. "He was right here when we started loading things."

"He went up the hill," said Pam, who notices everything.

I could feel Bill beginning to steam. "The boat is waiting," he said.

"Here he comes!" Jackie and Topper shouted.

"What were you doing?" I scolded. "We're ready to leave. Your dad was getting worried."

"I was climbing the tower," he said with a satisfied air.

"What tower?" Had the boy gone mad?

"You know, the communications tower."

"Here we are ready to leave and you're climbing a hundred-foot tower? You had better have a good reason."

"You remember that American flag I had?"

"Yes."

"Well! It's flying from the tallest point on Russell Island, in Moreton Bay, in Queensland, in Australia."

With everyone shouting, "Hurray, hurray!" there was no point of saying anything else.

"Fiddler's Green was just getting to be perfect," Pam sighed.

Bill put his arm around her. "But look at the legacy we're leaving behind. A street named American Avenue and an American flag flying above the highest point on the island." Laughing together, we watched the flag as it fluttered from the tower.

Saying goodbye to Fiddler's Green, our Australian Odyssey, we turned our faces toward the future. It was June 1973. There were new countries to see and new adventures to unfold.

As it faded from view, Topper waved one last time, "Goodbye, Russell Island. Goodbye, Gerard."

# Epilogue

## The Moores - Beyond Russell Island

The *You've Got To Be Kidding?* series covers a period of thirteen years. If you've read them all you have been with us as the older boys became adults and have known Topper from babyhood to grade school. The three girls fit nicely in between.

Our trip back to the States, full of adventures, allowed us to celebrate our greatest achievement yet. The Moores have circled the globe! In a zigzag fashion to be sure, but we actually can boast that we have been "around the world." It took eighteen months instead of 80 days, but—we did it!

Returning to the States, we settled in South Carolina near Bill's mother and sister. We suffered a major cultural shock when we realized the schools were teaching that "family" comes last.

"Your parents aren't always right," the children were told. "Their ideas are from a different era." We had returned in the middle of the "me generation."

A multi-million dollar high school, built near our home, had luxurious sports facilities but no auditorium for the arts. During our first month back, two neighborhood teens were abducted and killed by a murderer who had been newly released from prison.

"What have we gotten ourselves into?" we wondered.

Rusty, now a civilian, found ample work as a helicopter pilot, sometimes traveling to Europe for special jobs. Later, he was an instructor for fixed wing planes—until Skippy called him to a greater cause. This took him to Rhodesia where he became a Lieutenant in the Rhodesian Air Force.

Mickey did a two-year stint in the Navy before he satisfied his first love by graduating as a teacher and working with special needs students. Always the builder, he designed his own home. He did the finishing work himself, majoring in the latest gadgets such as remote-controlled ceiling fans, closet organizers and lights that turn themselves on when you enter a room.

Skippy chose "traveler" as his occupation. He covered a great deal of Europe. Hearing Rusty was on a crop-dusting job in Denmark, he found him before we had a proper address. After Europe, he traveled to South Africa to visit friends from our Proteia tour of 1973. Seeing the plight of landowners in Rhodesia, he came home to encourage his brother Rusty to join him. Until Rhodesia lost the war, they worked with the Air Force and militia to protect farmers' lands and their families.

Tia, always wanting to do the right thing, struggled with the change of standards and values in America. Because of her advanced Australian education, she was able to graduate a year early and entered Fashion Merchandising School. All the years we had spent pouring over patterns and materials were a great help in the course. With her talent for structure and design, she later became a civil engineer.

Pam, safely enrolled in a private school as an eighth grader, got more of an education than we expected.

"What's a prostitute?" she asked one day after school. When I wondered why she wanted to know, she told me she had one in her class. Curious Pam still knows where everyone is and what's going on. These skills have served her well in office management. "If you want to know something," the kids say, "ask Pam."

Jackie, a sixth grader in the same school, came home with the news that a girl in her class had drugs in her locker. Why was I not surprised?

"This is America," I told her. "Things are different." She understood that she couldn't solve everyone's problems, but she could still be kind and thoughtful.

Later, Jackie excelled in Public Relations. In the meantime, she and Pam devoted themselves to covering their bedroom door with red and blue winners' ribbons from Swim Meet Competitions.

Topper was less affected by the school's far-out behavior. Like his big brother Rusty, he learned to hunt and fish. As a hobby, he collected throw-away bicycles. An enterprising businessman, like his brother Mickey, he put the best parts together to make one good bike which he then sold. His ability to figure out a better way eventually led him into one of the most challenging branches of the U.S. Navy, the SEALS.

Did they all get married when they grew up? Yes, they did. All of them. We now have twenty grandchildren and one great-grandchild to be proud of. Watching the new generations develop their own uniqueness and talents, we have begun to understand life's deepest meaning. What we invested in our children is being reinvested in their children. From generation to generation, the Moore character and teachings live on.

# Russell Island - Beyond June 1973

Before we left, we put our property into the capable hands of Gerard McGee. His letters, and comments on events kept us well informed of island affairs. True to my prediction, property sales were headline news.

Land development continued. Glamorized publicity brought numbers of people over to the islands looking for a "paradise." On weekends, speedboats zipped back and forth bringing a stream of visitors. The barge was busy transporting passengers and their cars. All this activity often caused traffic jams at the jetty and on the roads. Weekenders camped wherever they could in tents or cars, often taking over the limited beach areas.

A number of islanders sold land to enjoy travel abroad. One islander didn't return home as expected. He had somehow landed in Singapore. It wasn't on his itinerary and no one could figure out how he got there.

But everyone was happily relieved when he finally made his way back home.

Over the months, new houses began springing up. With the increased population came a wave of vandalism. Several houses burned down. No one was able to determine the cause. Others were broken into. Some arrived on the island to find the block of land they had purchased under water. Many people abandoned their land. It was not the paradise they had expected from the advertisements.

In 1974, a big storm washed away roads and flooded a swamp, creating two islands instead of one. Campers, cars, and property owners were stranded on the south end of Russell. The road had to be rebuilt to get them back. For the first time on the islands, the Redland Shire Council levied rates (Australian for taxes). Taxes and fees didn't exist when we lived there.

During his ten months on the island, Gerard documented endless strife and dissension, often arising from the actions of the "bad seed." However, in spite of spats and quarrels, good things did happen.

Gerard found a pumpkin vine growing in the chook yard (Australian for chicken pen). "I thought I had pulled it all out," he wrote, "but it lived to travel on. Now I have pumpkins growing for miles." Later, he let us know that the avocado trees we planted in 1968 for our retirement were already bearing fruit.

We learned that all the island papaya trees had been killed by a disease. That is, except the ten that were growing on our property.

Gerard wrote, "Your trees have 'paw paws' as big as footballs. I'm keeping my eye on them." It was a nice tribute to our organic gardening.

Our house sold in April 1974, just ten months after we left. When the sale was final, our trusty caretaker went back to his cattle droving. He traveled to Sydney with a float belonging to the Prime Minister and flew back on the Prime Minister's DC9 jet. Returning to his hometown of Warwick, he settled near the nieces and nephews he loved so much.

"Have you ever been back?" we are often asked. I would have to say "no." One thing I've learned in life is: You can't go back. Life goes forward not backward. Things change. Russell Island, five by eight miles, is no exception. The latest statistics show a population of 3,000, compared to less than 200 when we were there. The tranquil life is no more. The exhilarating freshness of clean air is no more. All familiar landmarks are no more. Our house was one of those that burned down. Fiddler's Green no longer exists.

We were blessed to have lived in a moment of time when we had complete independence and freedom. We were able to develop our land and our children according to our values and our abilities. It was a challenge we welcomed. It was a challenge we answered well.

Russell Island was there for us when we needed it. For that, we will always be thankful. The memories held dear in our hearts and shared in this book-series will be passed down from generation to generation—a precious legacy. No, he wasn't kidding... Bill had found the best place to raise a family.

# Order Form

Moore Family Odyssey *You've Got to Be Kidding!* Series

❑ Book One:   *Move to Australia?*            ISBN 1-55306-438-0
❑ Book Two:   *Me? An Australian Farmer?*     ISBN 1-55306-637-5
❑ Book Three: *Sell Our Australian Farm?*     ISBN 1-55306-860-2
❑ Book Four:  *Tell Australia Goodbye?*       ISBN 1-55306-997-8

## Please print:

Name: _____

Address: _____

City: _____ State/Prov: _____

Zip/Postal Code: _____ Telephone: _____

_____ copies @ $14.95 US/$22.00 CDN.:       $_____

**Total amount enclosed:**                      $_____

Payable by Check or Postal Money Order

(Please make checks payable to Connie Moore.
Allow two to three weeks for delivery.)

**Send to:**        *Connie Moore*
                    12831 SE 97th Terrace Road
                    Summerville, FL  34491
                    USA